Malfred Ferndock's
MOREL
COOKBOOK

Peter Leach and
Anne Mikkelsen, Editors

FERNDOCK PUBLISHING

Ferndock Publishing
Box 86
Dennison, MN 55018

ISBN 0-9616321-0-0

this book is dedicated
to librarians. . .
computers may be user friendly,
but there's nothing like a librarian
who's interested in your project!

Contents

Part 1 - "It's still a little early. . ."

Part 2 - "We need some rain. . ."

After reviewing a rough draft, a friend remarked, "This is kind of a unique table of contents for a cookbook." Well. . .morels are unique! The difference between a morel cookbook and a carrot cookbook is a) there's not as much carrot lore around and b) not as many people seem anxious to read about carrots. On the other hand, those who hunt and savor morels "be much delighted with them," as Parkinson says about the Germanes. *A portion of that delight is often found in a good story. . .*

Recipes

HUGE FUNGUS — Possibly the largest morel of the season was found last Friday by Malfred Ferndock of rural West Dennison. The huge fungus, weighing 92 pounds, was found to be "a little tough" when a small sample was cooked. Ferndock plans to dry the giant mushroom and use it as a rabbit hutch.

Dennison Argus. May 28. 1953

Foreword

I wish I'd written this cookbook. In fact, I *had* originally planned to write it until a freak hunting accident made it impossible. As fate would have it, the accident occurred while I was hunting morels.

I have written elsewhere of the legendary *Morchella giganticus* (giant morel) and its strange disappearance in the early 1960s. Around here, these days, any morel weighing over a pound or two is cause for great excitement. However, if a person can get deep enough into an old woods. . .

11

Last Spring the boy (Bud) and I had gone to Northern Minnesota to hunt with two old friends, sisters by the way, who really "know the woods." We had found some five-to-seven pounders and were snaking a bunch of them up a slope to where the truck was parked. The cable snagged for a second on a stump and when it let go I caught that flying mess of morels square in the face. The Doc is at a loss to explain it, but ever since even the thought of morels gives me a nervous tic. He says he's sure it will pass by next Spring, but for now it's best if I take it real easy on anything having to do with morels.

This book might've been delayed a full year if two good neighbors hadn't volunteered to take over for me. Anne Mikkelsen has handled everything having to do with the recipes and Peter Leach dug up all of the morel lore.

There are plenty of field guides already and lots of cookbooks, too, so I gave 'em just one instruction: do a book I'd like to *read* on a cold winter's evening, sitting by the wood stove, thinking about spring. . .next year!

Malfred Ferndock
West Dennison, Minnesota

12

Preface

Overlooking the city of Parshall, North Dakota is a remarkable building made of stone. The Broste Rock Museum contains the creative life's work of one man, Paul Broste (1887-1975). There are paintings and a lapidary collection, but the most unique items are over 600 stone spheres which Broste made, as a hobby, during a lifetime of farming. In concluding a detailed description of sphere making he wrote, "After all is said and done, you have to cut spheres to learn to cut spheres."

This same bit of wisdom might be applied to morels: "You have to hunt morels to learn to hunt morels." It is my hope that the reader will learn a great deal about *cooking* morels and, beyond that, something of the pleasures of *hunting* morels, but it must be emphasized that this is not a field guide. I would strongly advise beginners against picking morels with this book as their only source of information. There is as much morel fiction as there is morel fact and the tyro should be cautioned that some contradictions will be found within these very pages. On the other hand, I hope that even the most experienced "morelist" will find, if not new information, at least several hours of pleasant reading.

Parts 1-4 are organized, albeit loosely, like the morel season itself. Morel hunters, although generally honest sorts, do tend to shade the truth a bit when morels are involved. Thus the statement, "It's still a little early..." really means, at the least, "I know where I could pick enough for supper..." Part 5 was an unexpected pleasure, since researching "holsome mushromes" was not a part of my original plan.

Unless otherwise credited, the illustrations are from the collection of this writer. The quotes which are scattered throughout the book have been collected over many years. (For some people morels are the *only* mushrooms and when they speak of "mushrooms," they mean morels.) Numerous individuals contributed suggestions, recipes, and, not least, information on "how to publish a book." I would like to again acknowledge the assistance of many librarians in my search for the elusive morel in print, especially Lee Ellison, Lothian Lynas, Maggie Rogers, and Joy Wolf.

In all honesty, I have not tasted the results of every recipe, but Anne has. Her enthusiasm for the subject and her culinary expertise are a guarantee that I will do so in the future! Thanks to all of you...

Peter Leach
Dennison, Minnesota

"It's a luxurious taste. It's elusive...mushroomy but much richer."

Introduction
Cooking with Morels

Ideas and suggestions for Malfred Ferndock's Recipe Contest were numerous and came from all parts of the country. My theory in regard to cooking and therefore in regard to recipe selection for the book, begins with the purity of the recipe. In this case, I was striving to maintain the flavor, dignity and prominence of the morel. On that premise, the first elimination of entries was made. Added to that is my strong feeling that any recipe should be receptive to the cook adding her or his own creativity and personal touch. Next, I began testing all remaining recipes and further eliminations were made. I read through Mushroom and Morel cookbooks and requested permission to reprint my favorites. A few recipes from restaurants rounded out my selections to the point where I feel quite confident any reader and cook can satisfy a hungry mob of morel lovers with the final selections presented in this book.

As I organized the recipes into a uniform format, the type of morel specified by the writer was retained. For some of the recipes, fresh, frozen, or dried morels would serve equally well. For others, such as stuffed morels, the fresh would be best. If your fresh morels are obviously clean, they need not be washed. If they appear dirty, rinse lightly or soak briefly.

Morels should not be eaten or frozen raw. For freezing, I heat about one pound (whole or sliced depending on size) over a medium-high heat for 6-7 minutes with 1 T. butter and no seasoning; the morels shrink to about one pint. Depending on the expected use, I freeze the resulting liquid with the morels or separately for stock. Morels may be dried on screens in a warm room or use a commercial dryer. If a handful of drying morels rattles sharply when shaken, they are ready to be stored in airtight containers. Several methods of reconstitution are suggested in the recipes. You may also use two 30 minute soakings in a minimum amount of cold water; reserve the liquid for stock.

Anne Mikkelsen
Northfield, Minnesota

Part 1
"It's still a little early. . ."

The Mystique of Morels
Judge Samuel R. Rosen

As well as anything I've read, this passage illustrates the "mystique of morels." One morel induces a dream and a subsequent mystical experience. . .even before it's picked! Sam Rosen is Judge of the 88th Judicial District (Brown County) State of Indiana. He has kindly authorized the printing of this excerpt from A Judge Judges Mushrooms *(Nashville, Indiana: The Highlander Press, 1982).*

People who know about locations where morels may grow rarely talk about them. Perversely, the morels do not grow each year in the same spot. For some reason that botanists have not fathomed, each year morels shift their beds to another, usually-nearby spot. Generally they are found and thrive in old apple orchards, near pine, elm and beech or in places where the ground has been burned. They are rarely found near oak trees. There is an exception to this, however, and the exception, which I will cite, was truly a mystical experience for this writer.

It was a beautiful spring day in Brown County in April 1976. Already there were stories that many people had found morels, but the tales were like "fish stories": there would either be a few morels found or bushels full. Anyway, I began my own search.

A friend and I had garnered information about several locations in which morels had been found in previous seasons. That first day we walked more than twenty miles, with little success. We noticed the May apples had begun to sprout, however. There were also "fiddle head" buds of ferns and wild onions all over. We gathered these in abundance, but, sadly, we found no morels.

That evening I informed my wife about our lack of success. I also solemnly vowed that if it rained during that night I would start bright and early the next day to begin again my hunt for the morels.

It did rain that night and I was very anxious to begin my hunt again. All through the evening I thought about what I was going to do the next day. When I retired I had a vivid and specific dream of finding a morel. The next morning after breakfast I felt a surge of optimism. I told my wife I felt confident I would find a morel.

My cabin is surrounded by oak, mostly white although there is some red oak. It is a most unlikely place to find morels. Nevertheless, over the past years I had always combed the area in the season and found a variety of other mushrooms. Never had I found a sign of a morel, but when I stepped out of the cabin that day to my amazement and wonderment I found that overnight there had grown a morel about six inches in height, no more than 15 feet from the house! The night before there could have been nothing in the same spot, because I had walked by it several times and had been observant.

I shouted to my wife. She came out and was as amazed as I had been. I called a neighbor and good friend, Cleve Porter, an excellent amateur photographer. He brought along his camera and took a picture for proof and posterity. It was an unusual experience which I feel had mystical overtones and is something I am pleased to relate.

"I promised I wouldn't make a scene if I found one. . . but I just couldn't help it."

The Merkle
Eugene J. McCarthy

Eugene McCarthy is a former U.S. Senator from Minnesota, where folks hunt morels. He now lives in Virginia, where he pursues the elusive "merkle." This essay has appeared in The Christian Science Monitor, *July 5, 1984 and* Mushroom, *Spring 1985. In authorizing its publication here, the author writes, "This past merkle season (1985) was very poor in Virginia, marked by more betrayals and evasions by other merkle hunters."*

I first heard of "the merkle" in September of 1979. I had just moved into my house in Rappahannock County, Va., at the foot of the Blue Ridge Mountains and was having my telephone installed. In the midst of technical telephone talk, the telephone man suddenly interrupted the discussion to ask whether I knew about the "merkles" on the ridge behind my house.

There was a note of awe in his voice. I first thought of people— "The Merkles." I said I didn't know them or of them. He went on to say that they came out in early April, and went on to explain and describe the location, weather conditions, dates, and other facts bearing on the coming and the finding of the merkles. I concluded as his exposition went on, that he was speaking of some kind of mushroom. He asked me whether he could come back in April to hunt for merkles. I assured him that he could.

In the course of the fall and winter, I made discreet inquiries about merkles among my neighbors. I raised the topic in the country store and at social gatherings. Nearly everyone I addressed on the topic said that they knew about merkles. Some said that they had eaten merkles and found them good. A few admitted to having collected them, but everyone seemed a little vague as to just when and where one might find merkles, or even, one merkle.

Distracted by the appearance of wood violets, bloodroot, May apples, and the buds on cherry trees—signs of spring I had known in Minnesota—I was not alert to the fact that the 1980 time of the merkle had come until one Sunday, in mid-April, I noted a few cars stopping in unusual places along Route 618, and persons, alone or in pairs, slipping out of the cars and then into the woods, some still dressed in their Sunday clothes, evidently having just come from church.

I concluded that the merkle waits for no man or woman, nor for a change of clothes, nor that it respected the Sabbath. I watched the woods edge, to note, hours later, the same persons, furtively coming out of the woods, clutching small brown bags, hurrying to their cars and disappearing down the road. I tried the woods on my own that first Sunday afternoon, and again the next morning, expecting to find merkles in great profusion, not unlike the manna of the desert. I found none. And gave up for the season.

1981 was a bad year for merkles in Rappahannock. Even experienced merkle hunters reported they had found none. The same was true of '82.

As April of 1983 approached, although I had doubts about the reliability of merkle hunters and their reports, I still had faith in the merkle. I was ready. I had gathered additional information about proper weather conditions for merkle growth. I had learned the relative advantages of seeking them under old apple trees, at the base of tulip poplars, adjacent to old pine stumps, and in some other less desirable locations. I had considered the relative advantage of the close-range, intensive search as against the cursive one; had considered the arguments made by some, reportedly successful, searchers of the east as against the west side of a ridge; and had even come to believe that possibly one should be dressed properly, a John Deere or an International Harvester cap, for example, and that, as some said, people with green or blue eyes were better able to see merkles in the debris of the woods than were those with brown eyes. My own bordered on brown.

I had no success in the 1983 season. But I was given a pint of merkles by one hunter as he crossed my yard after a successful hunt, and a promise that he would take me with him in the next season. The promise came from a resident of Culpeper County. He, in offering help to a resident of Rappahannock County, was a kind of latter-day Good Samaritan, and consistent with that biblical character he had offered to come back to help.

As this year's merkle season progressed, I waited, with greater and greater anxiety, for his return. He never came.

I decided to make one try for merkles on my own. And on the Saturday before Easter invited my neighbor, Dennis Fairbrother, to come with me. Dennis has blue eyes. He brought his two-year-old daughter, who also has blue eyes. I welcomed her, believing that the presence of innocence might help in the search for merkles. It did not.

Dennis and I went to a mountaintop Easter sunrise service the next morning. The horizon was clear as the sun rose, although, before the last minister had finished his remarks, it had clouded over. Each of the three speakers made reference to the certainty of the sunrise, of the coming of spring, of the blossoming of the redbud and of the wild cherry trees. I waited for some reference to merkles. There was none.

Back in my house after the service, I was resigned to accepting that another merkle season had come and gone. That I had failed again. Then my telephone rang. I thought for a moment that it might be the Culpeper County Samaritan. It was not. It was the wife of another neighbor, who together with her husband had been unsuccessful merkle hunters through many seasons.

"We've done it," she exulted over the phone. "Found merkles in our old orchard." Had they left any?

"No," she replied, but I could come over and look if I wished. I hurried over, and there in the orchard, I found one merkle, which either they had missed or which had sprung up after their passing. I picked it. My faith was saved. I will be ready for next year's season.

Simply Elegant! By far the most popular preparation for that "first pick of the season" burst of flavor is sauteed morels, served alone or with a cream reduction on toast.

Sauteed Morels
(2 servings)

1 dozen morels, halved. If washed, drain well first.
2 T. butter
½ tsp. lemon juice
salt
fresh cracked pepper

In a heavy-bottomed saucepan, melt the butter. Add the morels and lemon juice. Saute over medium heat 7-10 minutes, stirring now and then. Drain off the liguid and freeze for winter soup. Salt and pepper to taste.

Cream Sauce

1½ cup cream
1 recipe sauteed morels

Pour the cream into a heavy-bottomed saucepan and cook over medium heat to the boiling point. Adjust temperature to allow the cream to boil but not boil over. Reduce the cream by cooking to a thick consistency. Add sauteed morels and serve on toast.

"I once had the foolish idea that they grew next to stone walls, especially the corners of stone walls. You grab for any suggestion at all when you're looking for mushrooms."

My co-editor submitted his favorite morel recipe using Sauteed Morels in Cream Sauce and adding one more step.

Croissants Sogn

1 recipe of Sauteed Morels with Cream Sauce. If refrigerated over-night, the sauce will be a better consistency for filling.
1 croissant per person.

Slice each croissant so upper portion is 2/3. Remove the doughy inner portion of the roll. Fill the bottom portion with the morel filling. Replace top portion and bake 10 minutes at 350 degrees if filling is hot and 20 minutes if filling has been chilled.

Dr. Bloodmoney or
How We Got Along After the Bomb (Excerpt)
Philip K. Dick

Philip K. Dick (1928-1982) is one of America's best known science fiction writers. In the early Sixties, while living in Marin County, (Calif.) he became an avid mushroom collector and a member of the Mycological Society of San Francisco. Since morels are rare in Marin County and Dick never mentions them in his writing, I take a slight liberty in including my favorite author here. I am sure that Mr. Barnes, being recently from Oregon, would know morels... and their Latin names.[1]

Orion Stroud, chairman of the West Marin school board, turned up the Coleman gasoline lantern so that the utility school room in the white glare became clearly lit, and all four members of the board could make out the new teacher.

"I'll put a few questions to him," Stroud said to the others. "First, this is Mr. Barnes and he comes from Oregon. He tells me he's a specialist in science and natural edibles. Right, Mr. Barnes?"

The new teacher, a short, young-looking man wearing a khaki shirt and work pants, nervously cleared his throat and said, "Yes, I am familiar with chemicals and plants and animal-life, especially whatever is found out in the woods such as berries and mushrooms."

"We've recently had bad luck with mushrooms," Mrs. Tallman said, the elderly lady who had been a member of the board even in the old days before the Emergency. "It's been our tendency to leave them alone; we've lost several people either because they were greedy or careless or just plain ignorant."

Stroud said, "But Mr. Barnes here isn't ignorant. He went to the University at Davis, and they taught him how to tell a good mushroom from the poisonous ones. He doesn't guess or pretend; right, Mr. Barnes?" He looked at the new teacher for confirmation.

"There are species which are nutritious and about which you can't go wrong," Mr. Barnes said, nodding. "I've looked through the pastures and woods in your area, and I've seen some fine examples; you can supplement your diet without taking any chances. I even know the Latin names."

The board stirred and murmured. That had impressed them, Stroud realized, that about the Latin names.

"Why did you leave Oregon?" George Keller, the principal, asked bluntly.

The new teacher faced him and said, "Politics."

"Yours or theirs?"

"Theirs," Barnes said. "I have no politics. I teach children how to make ink and soap and how to cut the tails from lambs even if the lambs are almost grown. And I've got my own books." He picked up a book from the small stack beside him, showing the board in what good shape they were. "I'll tell you something else: you have the means here in this part of California to make paper. Did you know that?"

Mrs. Tallman said, "We knew it, Mr. Barnes, but we don't know quite how. It has to do with the bark of trees, doesn't it?"

This recipe has been praised by many morel devotees including Malfred Ferndock. It was submitted by Gaynell Schandel who has a flair for Mexican cooking.

Quesadillas con Hongos

Good flour tortillas, two or more per person
One slice monterey jack cheese per tortilla
3 T. sauteed morels per tortilla

Heat tortillas one or two at a time on a "comal" (tortilla griddle) or in a frying pan, turning with a spatula. Place a slice of cheese on the tortilla, fold in half, and continue to turn until the cheese begins to melt. Fill with 3 T. sauteed morels and place in a warm oven until you have a sufficient quantity for serving.

Uncovenanted Mercies (Excerpt)
Edward Hyams

For a number of years Edward Hyams (1912-1975) wrote a column entitled "In an English Garden" for The Illustrated London News. *This excerpt appeared in the May 21, 1960 issue and is reprinted with permission from The Illustrated London News Picture Library. As an aside, in the January 5, 1889* Review of Applied Natural Sciences M. le Baron d'Yvoire *writes, "This sympathy of morels for apple residue has already been noted by several mycologists."*

I was going to write about lilacs this week. But there has been an event in my garden which has turned my attention to the subject of the occasional "free gifts," as the advertising agents say in their tautological way, which a garden makes to a gardener. We have been presented, out of the blue, with a crop of morels.

The collection of household rubbish being as unsatisfactory here as in many country districts, we are in the habit of digging, from time to time, a large square hole in some unvisited part of the paddock, into which the dustbin can be emptied, and which is, in due course, covered over with soil and turf. Yesterday afternoon I was hand-weeding our still very raw-looking new "wild" garden, admiring the flowers on the new evergreen azaleas, and looking for lily shoots—L. pardalinum, L. martagon and L. formosanum are through, but of the others there is no sign as yet—when my wife, crossing a part of the paddock which took her past an old rubbish pit which had been filled in and covered about six months ago, called to me to come and look at some extraordinary objects which had appeared all over it. I regret to say that neither of us recognised them. I went to look, and together we examined them— a number of large, hard, handsome but slightly sinister-looking fungi which we had never seen before. (Actually, we must have done, but in the dried and unrecognisable form in which they are sold in French foodshops and on French market stalls.)

I dug one up and examined the material beneath it: I was very surprised indeed to find the hyphae running densely through a clotted mass of charred newspaper, debris of a not very successful

NURTURED ON *THE TIMES* (CHARRED) AND THE PULP FROM A CIDER PRESS: MORELS (*MORCHELLA ESCULENTA*), WHICH APPEARED IN MR. HYAMS' PADDOCK AS AN " UNCOVENANTED BLESSING." THE LARGER IS 9 INS. TALL. (*Photograph by Douglas Weaver.*)

fire. The fungi appeared to be nourishing themselves on that un-promising pabulum, and on nothing else. Some of them may have had their hyphae down into the last rubbish which had been thrown into the pit, the dried must from the cider press: we have stopped using that on the compost heaps owing to the forest of apple seed-lings which spring up in the compost later; the germ of the pips does not seem to be destroyed by the heat of either fermentation or composting. But there is no doubt that most of the fungi, some of which were 9 ins. tall and 6 ins. through the widest part of·the corky, folded and pitted caps, were growing on a "soil" of burnt newspapers.

We were going to have coffee with a naturalist friend after dinner that evening, and it was he who, delighted with our find, identified the fungi as *Morchella esculenta*, the *morille* of French gastronomy, the morel which was formerly much eaten in England, but which, our friend told us, he had only once before seen growing in this country during the past twenty years. Our morels are confined strictly to the 5-ft. square of the rubbish pit top. Consulting the Penguin "Edible Fungi," by John Ramsbottom, we discovered that the caps may be "ochraceous yellow," or in other cases, "blackish grey to brown." Ours were of the more sombrely coloured kind. I entertained the fancy that this might be because they were growing on *The Times*; I can think of four or five newspapers which, by the same token, would give rise to the "ochraceous yellow" sort. Mr. Ramsbottom also says that morels have been noted "on charred paper, rubbish, and apple pulp from cider factories." In our pit they had all three. But the pleasant mystery is, how on earth did the spores find this favored medium? I have never seen morels in the parish—or anywhere else for that matter. And our naturalist friend seemed to think they are rare.

Such incidents as this give to gardening that touch of surprise which can not, of course, be one of the pleasures of planned cultivation. And they persuade you to be not merely a gardener, but a plantsman and a naturalist, if only because they send you to books for explanations of discoveries.

"What's the worst thing that can happen? If you are out in the woods and don't find any mushrooms, well, at least you are out in the woods."

This recipe was submitted by Don James of Glendale, Arizona, who is unable to find morels in Arizona, but developed the recipe while living in Iowa, where morels are plentiful.

Morels au Vin
¼ pound butter
1 clove garlic, pressed
3 T. minced onion
1 lb. morels
salt and pepper to taste
¼ cup sauterne wine

28

Melt the butter in a frying pan over low heat. Add the garlic and onion. Cut morels in half and add to onion. Saute until morels and onions are tender. Add sauterne and simmer until wine is cooked down and covers only the bottom of the pan. Enjoy!

Always Look Twice
Ron Schara

The following bit of doggerel originally appeared in Ron Schara's outdoor column in the Minneapolis Star and Tribune, *May 5, 1985. It is printed here, with his permission, "as written by Ron Schara, since that is not my real name."*

Basswood clumps are worth trying,
And apple orchards need a look.
And veteran seekers swear by the book
That Dutch Elm victims, whose bark is loose,
Is where morels grow thick
around on the ground.

Warm nights and warmer rains that fall
Are the surest May signs
Of morels growing tall.
But don't be misled by forests disasters,
morels grow in burns
as well as cow pastures.

One final word, some morel advice.
If you find one mushroom growing,
that's awfully nice.
But the fungi is gregarious; sharing
spores is no vice.
Keep your eye on the spot
Always look twice.

Hunting the Wild Morel
Ida Geary

This is probably the ideal way to begin one's morel hunting career: take a chartered bus to a known location, in the company of experienced hunters, and end the day with a 2:30 P.M. happy hour. Ida Geary described her "initiation" in the May 1982 California *magazine; reprinted with permission from that publication.*

For a few hours last spring, after I had eaten the nine small morel mushrooms I found at Pinecrest, I wondered if they would have any effect on me. Whenever you eat a new wild mushroom, there is always a slight doubt as to whether it will agree with you. Even the varieties with which you are familiar can disagree with you inexplicably on occasion, but if you are a true wild mushroom aficionado, you will never attribute your discomfort to the mushrooms. Instead, you will believe it was due to some other aspect of the meal—the rich dessert, perhaps, or too much wine. After all, as one wild mushroom lover said to me, you get sick even if you never eat wild mushrooms.

So I was relieved after an interval to realize I was going to be happy with my first morels. I had heard so much about this legendary delicacy that when Larry Stickney of the Mycological Society of San Francisco organized a bus trip to Pinecrest Lake (a little north of Yosemite National Park) to search for the honey-combed-cap beauties, I was out of my house at 5:15 A.M. that Saturday morning and on the bus leaving downtown San Francisco at 6 A.M. sharp.

Once off the bus people fanned out, equipped with baskets, waxed paper, and lunches, and they seemed to disappear into the landscape, some off to secret spots they knew about from previous seasons. At first I was happy just to be there. It was a beautiful warm day in the Sierra—the white clouds floating in the blue sky and the brightly shining sun were mirrored in the sparkling mountain lake. The air smelled like pine, nesting birds were singing, and the company was pleasant. But after a half hour or so I wanted to see a legendary morel. Not only was I, a beginner, not finding any, but there were also no cries of joy from the experienced members of our small party.

Suddenly one person stopped, exclaiming, and turned to collect two obscure brownish morels in the shade of a rounded white granite rock. I stopped, too, and saw a morel almost under one of her feet. In bird-watching circles, and also in wildflower watching, both of which I have some experience with, it would not do to snatch a prize from under someone else's nose, or foot. But in mushroom hunting, Larry Stickney assured me, it was all right for me to collect that morel, and so I did. I carefully put it into a waxed paper envelope and into my little basket.

Now I had my first morel, and I began to feel a little more hopeful, but in the long interval until I found the second one, I started to call it my $15 morel. That was the cost of the bus trip.

The trouble with morel hunting in the high forest is that the hollow, honeycombed, pointed-top morels are almost the same size, color, and shape as two-or three-inch ponderosa pinecones. On the darkened forest floor—covered with brown pine needles and cones, black oak and cottonwood leaves—one needs a practiced eye to sort out the occasional morel from the hundreds of cones. And my eye was not yet practiced. I could see the shy yellow violets and the pink bell-shape flowers on the manzanita bushes and even the tips of the red snow plant pushing up through patches of melting snow. But I couldn't seem to see any morels. As one person put it, it was like looking for Easter eggs that nobody had put out.

But soon Larry generously pointed out two small morels for me to pick as he went up the bank after some others, and that served to encourage all of us. It also brought the price of my three mushrooms down to $5 each—a little better, but not exactly a bargain.

By 2:30 P.M., when we stopped hunting to gather round a well-provided picnic table for happy hour, I had nine morels in my basket. Although one hateful, sharp-eyed, experienced hunter had found 60, I was feeling proud of myself. I had enough of the little beauties for a small Sunday lunch the next day, and the price, while still high, had gone down considerably from that first expensive and not quite honest find.

On the way home I sat next to Salvatore Billeci, one of the old-timers of the Mycological Society, and later I cooked the morels as he suggested—the simplest way, sauteed in butter and served on toast. This way, he pointed out, you get the full flavor of the morels, although there are all kinds of elaborate ways of cooking them. Sal Billeci loves morels so much he has been trying to cultivate them for the last twenty years, but so far to no avail. The first one to cultivate morels, he says, will have his fortune made.

No one has ever been able to describe to me what the morel tastes like. People just say they are "wonderful" or "like nothing else" while smiling knowingly as older girls do when asked by younger girls about love. But now that I have had my first taste, I can say that morels are tender, and they are sweet—they taste nothing at all like commercial mushrooms. As a matter of fact, they are "wonderful" and taste "like nothing else," just as they were described to me.

This recipe for Cream of Morel Soup comes from the Tapawingo Restaurant in Ellsworth, Michigan, courtesy of the owner and chef, Harlen "Pete" Peterson. Reprinted courtesy of the Charlevoix County Press, Boyne City, Michigan.

Tapawingo Cream of Morel Soup
(serves 4 generously)

½ pound fresh morels, small if possible
2 T. unsalted butter
salt and freshly ground pepper
4 cups rich homemade chicken stock (grease removed)
4 egg yolks
1 cup heavy cream

Clean, and remove stems of morels, if they are tough. Cut into spoon-sized pieces if they are large. Heat butter in saucepan, then add morels, salt and pepper; cover and let simmer for about 10 minutes. Add the stock and bring just to the boil. Meanwhile, mix together the egg yolks and the cream. Slowly add this mixture to the morels, never allowing the soup to come to the boil (it would curdle). Correct the seasoning with salt and pepper, and a few drops of lemon juice, if desired.

Thank you to ROON by Jerry Petermeier and John Ratzloff for the following tempura recipe. We especially enjoyed the light crunch of the batter. (See page 109 for ordering information.)

Morel Tempura

1½ cups tempura batter: 1 cup flour
                              3 T. cornstarch
                              1 T. oil
                              9 T. lukewarm water
1 cup halved, medium size fresh morel caps
1 green pepper, chopped to same size as morels
1 red pepper, chopped to same size as morels
1 onion, chopped in large pieces
2 stalks celery, cut to same size as morels
1 zucchini, cut to same size as morels
½ lb. shrimp, about the same size as morels, cleaned but with
      tails intact
1 bunch parsley

Mix the first three ingredients of the batter and add the lukewarm water slowly, mixing gently to form a smooth batter. Let the batter rest a few minutes while you heat deep frying oil to 350 degrees and prepare the other ingredients. Wash and dry the morels and other vegetables and shrimp with paper towels. Dip morels and other vegetables and shrimp into batter one at a time and shake off excess batter gently. Carefully lower battered morels into the hot oil and continue to cook each item. The cooked pieces can be passed immediately to guests around the table or an alternative presentation is to fry the food in batches, keeping the cooked pieces on a cookie sheet on paper towels in a 250 degree F. oven. When all food is fried, serve the entire platter.

An excellent dipping sauce can be made by mixing ½ cup vinegar, ½ cup soy sauce, 1 tsp. chili oil and ½ cup minced scallions.

Part 2
"We need some rain. . ."

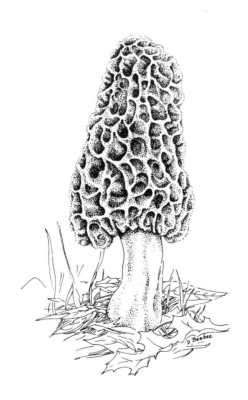

The morelist
Justin Isherwood

In order to protect his whereabouts, I will say only that Justin Isherwood is a farmer living in central Wisconsin. . .and his Fire Number is 5324. "The morelist" originally appeared in Wisconsin Natural Resources, *May-June 1979; reprinted with the author's permission.*

When lilacs in the dooryard bloom. When planting is finally finished and the ambitious seed is in warming ground. When the plowshares are at last let cool and an ease comes over the township.

Then is a time when the farmer can come to know his woods again and see what the spring has brought.

There is a ritual of the woods that occurs from mid-May to early June—a ritual of Sunday morning walks, hunting morel mushrooms. In this religion, two sects exist, mushroomers and morel mushroomers. The difference is one of ability.

The mushroomer can cipher the form and texture that identify the eatable from the noneatable. In the world of mushrooms the distinction is sharp between palatable and poisonous, or if you prefer the hard edged words, between the living and the dead.

The mushroomer is a courageous sort. It is an act of wonder to watch one go to a patch of sylvan agaricus (which look like little white umbrellas with lace drip collars), pick a bushel basket full, take them home, throw them in a quick pressure cooker and can a winter supply.

The mushroom identification book has a picture of sylvan agaricus with the big word "edible" beneath it. Next to it is another picture of the flat-capped agaricus (which also looks like a little white umbrella with a lace drip collar). Beneath is the word "Poisonous."

The true mushroomer will scoff at that and say they aren't really poisonous. "Ah well, they might make you a little sick but they're not poisonous." They might make a mushroomer a little sick, the rest of us normal mortals they would probably kill.

But mushrooming isn't all that bad and one of the reasons is the existence of the morel. That plant alone proves this is a loving universe. The morel is a delicacy of the multitude. If you can't tell the difference between a daisy and a rutabaga you can still distinguish a morel from a host of other mushrooms.

The morel looks like a pointed sponge three to five inches in height. A pitted conical head sits atop a creamy white stalk of half its total length. Color of the head varies from tan (light brown) to brown (dark tan) or grayish. At emergence they tend to have their darkest color, which fades in the few days of its existence to a gray almost white head.

For the morel mushroomer the picking spot is both secret and · holy ground. It is too much to ask of a friend that he would tell the whereabouts of his morel ground. Perhaps it is too much to ask even of a marriage partner.

Some local farmers have been seen heading into the woods on a fine clear Sunday morning while wife and kids dressed for church, with the excuse of mending fence, a frying pan slung over one shoulder, a small pat of butter in the jacket pocket and a couple matches.

There is a theological theory that the forbidden fruit in the garden was in fact morel mushrooms, that the maker wanted to save the flavor (and knowledge) for himself, herself or itself.

The place to hunt that musty tidbit is in old woods. There are those who say to look for ash trees and there you will find the best morel ground. There are those who say go among the old dead elms.

Some say don't look at all if it hasn't rained recently, that dry ground and mushrooms don't go together. There is plenty of evidence that few can be morelists when it really gets hot.

Others go into the hills to find the deserted homestead with an old apple orchard out back. Still others look only beneath balsam fir and others hunt in mature oak woods.

The true morelist will find them almost anywhere, making the best of a nearby world.

Morels are never abundant and thus difficult to share. Like too many good things, they don't respond well to cultivation. You can't just throw the seed in the ground and wait then for an easy harvest like prayers thrown at a vending machine deity. You have to go on the search yourself and find the knowledge and delight of the woods.

There is an ethic involved. You should ask whose woods these are. Not many do that anymore (if they ever did)—come to the door, hat in hand and ask in mild voice if it is OK.

Not many come on that hot Saturday afternoon to help pack away the last of the hay in the hot, thin aired mow and sit afterwards talking easy on the porch with a cold beer before milking time. If so, there would be fewer of those big yellow signs with black letters saying "NO TRESPASSING." At least they would know it wasn't meant for them!

One more thing, the morelist doesn't pick them all. Some are left if not for others then out of humility—that we would not be like an ancient king who shot arrows at the sun in an attempt to kill it. There is an Iroquois tale which says that king was the father of the white race.

Enough of this, go find morels for yourself. If you don't find any you will no doubt visit their green neighbors and that is reward enough in spring.

We found this recipe to be the morel spread best highlighting the subtle morel flavor. It was submitted by Diane Dare of Evansville, Indiana.

Morel Spread

¼ cup butter
1 cup chopped morels
½ cup butter
2 T sour cream
¼ tsp. salt
dash pepper
4 T. sherry

Melt ¼cup butter, saute morels, cool. Combine morels, any juice, ½ cup butter and rest of ingredients in blender or food processor. Blend until smooth, about a minute. Chill slightly before serving.

"I like the timber. . .and I just like to be out. I'd just as soon be doing this as anything I can think of."

Thank you Carol Scott from Wabasha, Minnesota for the following Quiche recipe.

Morchella Quiche with Veggies
(Serves 6)

½ dozen morels sliced
2 small zucchini, thinly sliced
1 scallion, sliced
1 medium clove garlic, minced
¼ cup butter
1 tomato, chopped
½ cup green pepper, chopped
soy sauce to taste
¼ tsp. pepper
¼ tsp. each basil and thyme
9" pastry shell, partially baked
3 eggs
3/4 cup half and half
½ cup parmesan cheese

Saute morels, zucchini, scallion and garlic in butter about 5 minutes, stirring occasionally. Stir in tomato, green pepper, soy sauce, pepper, basil and thyme. Cook over low heat 10-15 minutes or until vegetables are tender and liquid has evaporated. Spread mixture evenly in pastry shell. Beat eggs together with half and half until mixed but not frothy, pour over vegetables. Sprinkle with parmesan cheese. Bake in preheated 375 degree oven 30-35 minutes or until knife inserted near center comes out clean.

Jottings

Jim Silbar

If morel hunting has a mecca, it must be Boyne City, Michigan. The chief chronicler of activities there is Jim Silbar, Editor of the Charlevoix County Press. . .*in which these notes appeared May 11, 1983. (The* Sports Illustrated *article referred to may be found in the May 14, 1984 issue.)*

I finally found out how to find those morel mushrooms. After two years of trying, I finally found at least one hidden in the leaves someplace along the side of a hill in Chandler Township. With the finding of that mushroom, I also learned the secret to finding that one and a whole lot more of them too. All it takes is to walk back into the woods during the National Mushroom Championships and find Tony Williams. That is the secret.

After you find him, then do like I did, watch how the four-time national champion works an area, running, yes, running, along the hill, looking for those little things. You have to run to gather the mushrooms Tony has in order to win. But Tony doesn't cover the ground as well as he could if he were not in a hurry. And that is where I found my first patch of morels.

You see, Tony was working this area, and a guy from *Sports Illustrated* was trying to take pictures of him as he jumped around looking for the morels when I caught up with him. He moved on after finding a few in the area where we were trying to get his picture. We stayed in the area figuring that if we moved too much farther, we would get lost. Lo and behold, I found I was almost standing on top of a morel. I would not have noticed it myself, but the guy from the magazine said that there was one right next to my foot. After looking for a couple of seconds, I was indoctrinated in the sport of mushrooming. I found it. And then I found another, and he found another, and I found one, and so on.

Dave Guzniczak from the little daily up the road was with us and he found a bunch of them, too. And the best thing was that both of the guys didn't want to keep the mushrooms they found, but they kept putting them in my bag for my eating. It seems that Tony, in his hurry to find enough to win, glossed over the section we were standing in, content to take about twenty and then figuring that there was a better spot somewhere else farther back in the hills. He missed quite a few and we found them. Boy, were they good when I ate them.

Now, next year, I think I am going to enter the contest, especially now that I know what they look like, how they stand up in the woods, and almost everything.

As I see it, I have only one problem. The darn things have to be growing around my feet as I walk through the woods so I can find 'em.

Wild Mushroom Recipes by Carole Eberly has a good recipe for mushrooms and wild rice. Since we are using morels and wanted to enhance their flavor, we chose to use chicken stock instead of the suggested beef stock. (See page 110 for ordering information.)

Morels and Wild Rice
(Serves 6)

1 cup morels
2 T. butter
2 cups chicken stock
1 minced onion
½ cup wild rice
1 cup long-grain rice
2 T. chopped parsley

Quarter the morels and saute with onions in butter for 5 minutes. Bring chicken stock to a boil. Add wild rice and morel mixture. Reduce heat, cover and simmer 20 minutes. Add long-grain rice. Boil again. Reduce heat again. Cover and simmer 20 minutes, or until done. Mix in parsley just before serving.

A person can become ticked off after a day in the woods
Ron Schara

Often journalists' accounts of morels and morel hunting are remarkably similar, since they have encountered their first morel just prior to putting paper into the typewriter. Ron Schara, however, wrote in a more recent outdoor column, "As a kid, I was raised on picking morels and picking wood ticks." The following column appeared in the Minneapolis Star and Tribune, *May 20, 1982; reprinted with permission.*

I happened into a discussion about wood ticks the other day. It's an awful subject. One mention of the word and all within earshot start scratching. Try it sometime at a party.

Next to actually finding one, the worst feeling is to *think* that a wood tick may be crawling on your body.

People with hairy bodies probably suffer most. This is because a wood tick, in search of thin skin for parasitical purposes, will invariably try to crawl over these hairy spots.

If the hairy person is not preoccupied, the wood tick may be detected as it clumsily tries to walk eight-legged up a fuzzy thigh.

The problem is hairy people more than others also tend to imagine they feel the patter of tick feet.

But what's really amazing is that some wood ticks can go the length of a hairy person's body without ever being found out. How they do it, I don't know.

"Would you believe I had a wood tick buried in my belly button one time," John Clark said.

"I didn't know it for days. I mean, who looks at their belly button on a daily basis?"

"I only found it by accident," Clark went on. "I was standing in the shower soaping up when I felt this lump on my stomach. Had to go to the doctor to have it removed. The doctor said he'd never seen a wood tick in a belly button before."

My brother, Robert, still has a knot on the top of his head, the result of a tick bite that happened about 20 years ago.

Frankly, there's no easy way of removing a buried wood tick. It's a problem that has inspired more suggestions than a case of bad breath.

Some medical experts say use a tweezer or a piece of cotton and gently pull (don't yank) the tick until it backs out. Others suggest covering the tick with an oily substance, such as kerosene, salad oil, mineral oil, lighter fluid and so forth. The oily covering tends to suffocate the tick, forcing it to back out. But sometimes, the experts say, it's necessary to leave the oil on the tick for 30 minutes or more.

Tell me. Could you sit still for half an hour knowing a wood tick was tapped into your blood supply?

My own pet method was to hold a hot match or lighted cigarette near the tick.

The subject of wood ticks came up when somebody mentioned the joys of hunting morel mushrooms in Minnesota. The tasty sponge-like morel grows in the woodlands following the first warm rains of May.

Exactly where the morels may be found is information seldom shared among mushroom enthusiasts and certainly not with newcomers.

Veteran morel pickers will go to any length to discourage competition, although they are often subtle about it.

The morel mushroom season has begun. So has the season for ticks.

The State Mushroom
Herb Harper

Before retiring, Herb Harper taught biology at the Forest Lake (Minn.) High School. He has hunted mushrooms in China and the Soviet Union and is the author of Harper's Mushroom Guide and Check List. *(See page 113 for ordering information.) In this article, originally printed in the Fall 1984* Mushroom, *he reveals how Minnesota became the first state to designate a State Mushroom.*

Last year at a board meeting of our Minnesota Mycological Society (second oldest in the U.S.) someone suggested that a state mushroom would help publicize the society. In February 1983 I called our state senator, Gary Laidig, who wondered if I was really serious.

I wrote him to explain that I certainly was, and provided background information on morels. A bill was drafted, though it never came to vote in the 1983 legislature. Newspaper articles appeared in St. Paul and Minneapolis, and there was a letter to the editor from a disgruntled taxpayer who felt tax money was being frittered away by wacky legislators who should have more important matters to attend to.

One problem was to get legislators to *pronounce* morel correctly. There was much joking in the legislative halls, associating the proposed state mushroom with the so-called "moral majority."

Then too, there were a few hushed comments in our mycological society that we would be attracting all those out-of-staters to pick *our* mushrooms, and that local people would find their secret morel spots invaded. ("Better to keep morels a secret.") One society member wrote to Sen. Laidig expressing her opposition and charging that there was no official backing from the Minnesota Mycological Society because the entire membership had not voted.

Most society members, however, welcomed the publicity and saw no great threat to their secret mushrooming places.

This last spring we got the ball rolling again. Some other members of the society and I, along with Sen. Laidig, testified before the Senate Agricultural and Natural Resources Committee for about an hour. I tried to make an ecological point about *good*

fungi, and a commercial point about how tourism could bring dollars into the state. I pushed the fact that life on planet earth could very well exist without humans, but not without fungi. (Newspapers look for something sensational.)

Later there was a hearing before the House committee, whose members good-naturedly chided Rep. Connie Levi (a supporter of the bill, and a morel picker) as to whether the morals of the populace would be improved by the bill. Legislators who associate fungi with "ishy, rotting things" looked at me quizzically, but Rep. Levi and a few other legislators who were morel pickers were eager to tell about the times they had made a big find.

The bill was passed this spring and signed by Gov. Rudy Perpich, producing additional newspaper articles and radio and TV coverage. Mushroom hunters may forget that the majority of people buy their mushrooms in plastic containers, if they eat them at all, and lack the interest to learn anything about wild mushrooms.

"If the morel becomes the state mushroom, the sale of these delectable fungus plants should be forbidden."

45

From *A Judge Judges Mushrooms* by Judge Samuel R. Rosen comes this recipe for using morels in a popular pasta preparation. (See page 109 for ordering information.)

Tetrazzini
(serves 6)

1 six ounce package of fine spaghetti
6 T. butter
3 cup sliced morels
½ cups chives, finely chopped
3 T. flour
1½ tsp. salt
½ tsp. freshly ground pepper
2 cups hot milk
¼ cup dry sherry
1/3 cup chopped parsley
1½ cups mozzarella cheese cut into small pieces

Cook spaghetti until just tender in a large pot of boiling salted water. Drain and pour into a buttered large, shallow oven-proof dish. Cover with foil and set aside to keep warm. In a three-quart saucepan melt butter and cook morels and chives over medium heat until tender, about 5 minutes. Then over low heat add flour, salt and pepper, blending smoothly into the butter. Continue to cook; gradually add milk, then sherry. Continue to cook a moment or two longer, add parsley and a cup of cheese, reserving the rest. When cheese has melted, remove from heat. Pour sauce over the spaghetti in the oven-proof dish and spread with the remaining half-cup of cubed cheese. Broil 10-12 inches from the heat until the spaghetti and sauce are hot and the cheese is melted. *Watch carefully.* Serve at once.

"They're elusive little rascals. You have to walk slowly to spot them before they spot you, or they'll get up and run away from you."

Hymn to the Morel
F. Leuba

*This is an excerpt from a copy of a translation of an excerpt...
the details of which follow. The "original" copy was printed in
the May 1980* Mycena News, *published by the Mycological Society
of San Francisco.*

In the Wassons' *Mushrooms, Russia & History* is an excerpt
from a piece by a Swiss pharmacist and mycologist of the last
century (F. Leuba) presented untranslated because as the Wassons
said, "in the rarefied world of mycophiles to whom we offer our
book, are we not safe to assume that many read French?"

The Mycological Society of Toronto has published a translation of this exuberant piece in its April issue of "The Mycelium"—
and Larry Stickney made copies of it for us:

"Here is the morel! Does not the very name conjure delicious
memories of happy picking, enchanted walks, the smell of pine,
pinkish clouds of dawn...and the whole intoxicating procession
of springtime? Whose heart doesn't quiver joyfully remembering
the form of one of those beautiful morels, that you contemplated
for a moment before daring to bring it down with a sacriligious
hand? Who doesn't know the morel, and who, knowing it, does
not love it? Of all the mushrooms, no other thrills the amateur as
much, no other is sought with as much passion and relentlessness,
or interests so many different kinds of people. From the business-
man to the idle rich, the artist to the laborer, all love to find it.
I know individuals who during morel season, allow themselves
ten to fifteen consecutive days for their hunt, crossing the (land)
from one end to the other and often with very rewarding results."

Joe Walker of Castro Valley, California suggested this winning recipe.

Vegetable and Morel Dressing for Fish

½ cup butter
½ cup finely chopped onions
½ cup finely grated carrots
½ cup or more chopped raw morels
3/4 cup minced parsley
½ cup dry bread crumbs
1 egg, beaten
1 tsp. salt
Pepper to taste

Mix all ingredients together. Pack lightly around fish. If you are using a whole fish, pack some into the cavity. Bake at 350 degrees **until fish is done.**

"It's nice hunting morels . . .they start growing in the spring when everything else is budding. And it's just nice to walk in the woods. Coming back with a bag of mushrooms is just icing on the cake."

Etiquette for the Morelly Wanting
Ms. Mushroom

These rules appeared in the Summer 1984 Mushroom *as "Etiquette"
by Ms. Mushroom. The manuscript received from Lorelei Norvell
of Portland, Oregon bears the title "Ms. Mushroom's Guide to the
Morelly Inept." Now another editor has had his way with the title;
the rules remain the same.*

"As winter snows trickle through the gutters, one may be given
to contemplation of pleasant spring mornings spent in the company
of Dear Friends while stalking morels. Because one may be ignorant
of the proper mushroom etiquette presiding over these little ex-
cursions, Ms. Mushroom offers ten rules to the morel novice. If,
in the future, one should ever encounter awkward situations not
covered by this modest proposal, Ms. Mushroom graciously con-
sents to answer any queries regarding the Art of Mushrooming."

1. Should one have the uncommonly good fortune to be invited
on a morel stroll for the first time, it is considered bad form to
appear empty-handed in the morning in anticipation of equal division of the booty at day's end. No, gentle reader, one is expected
to have one's own small sturdy basket in hand which signals to
one's host serious hard-working intent. A large basket is not ad-
vised for this first trip with one's bosom companion, because that
may tend to give one's host Second Thoughts. One is not there to
rape, pillage or mutilate the forest serene. One is there to appre-
ciate the beauty of the moment and perhaps, if so invited, take a
few treasured remembrances home with one.

2. Before one gathers in a mushroom field, one must first Ask Permission. One does not invade privately owned property for the
procurement of delight without first locating the owner to solicit
hospitable acquiescence. Unfortunately, because past courtesies
have not been extended and the rightful owners have frequently
been ignored, the offender might possibly share the fate of the
Tillamook Ten (one too horrible to grace the pages of this restrained
publication). One will of course also acknowledge and honor all

rules of Park and Forest, no matter how imbecilic they may appear. Ms. Mushroom sympathizes with the Enthusiastic, but Park Rules state quite clearly that growing flora shall not be hacked down for the purpose of acquiring the morel growing at the Center.

3. Should one encounter what is termed a "morel garden" while at a fellow mushroomer's side, one is encouraged to drop to one's feet and engage in a diffident murmur and gentle lifting motion. It is considered ill form to dash before one's compatriot to sweep the entire contents of the garden into one's own basket. However, should one be confronted by a garden of 100 or so morels while momentarily alone, one is permitted to gather the first eighty or so specimens before alerting one's bosom companion as to its existence. It is wise for one to leave at least one or two fresh, non-rotten morels in the remaining twenty. It is also considered bad form to uproot trees or strike down elderly companions in the rush to reap one's allotted twenty when one's bosom companion signals that he himself has discovered a garden of his own. A simple ankle-turning lunge will suffice.

4. Some controversy has revolved around whether one may pluck a mushroom with one's fingers or whether one must use a trowel or knife to slice the stem off at ground level. Ms. Mushroom feels that presuming one is relatively confident that the mushroom one is holding is in fact a morel and not a deadly Amanita, one may use either fingers or implement. However, slicing all inedible portions of the morel to leave the remnants in a conspicuous heap near the erstwhile morel patch is considered rubbing the noses of the less fortunate in their ill-timing. One should instead disguise one's good fortune by covering those remnants with twigs, leaves or earth. This preserves the environment while simultaneously encouraging one's worthy competitors to think that morels don't live there anymore.

5. Ms. Mushroom is adamant in her condemnation of the Russula Stomp. While all morellers become justifiably provoked at the persistence of the Ubiquitous Russula or Maggoty Bolete, one must refrain from venting one's frustration upon the innocent non-morel. Much better to pass silently along, carefully covering all traces of any morel one does find. This will more than ever convince the unsuspecting that nature's pristine beauty has not been sullied and morels in this vicinity are a Thing of the Past.

6. Ms. Mushroom beseeches the uninitiated to return always the mycelial layers to their original state as closely as possible. Unfortunately, many morellers feel it is their unalienable right to employ sticks, canes, rakes or shovels to overturn any matter which might possibly conceal the elusive morel, leaving behind a path of destruction in their wake. Not only is this highly improper and a complete outrage to the Polite Mushroomer, it is destructive to future crops. Such ignorance should not be tolerated, and all vigilant and courteous morellers are expected to take immediate Retaliatory Action (See Rule #10).

7. One must show an enlightened sense of responsibility to one's fellow wo/man. One should not tangle oneself in the lines of a fishpole when in the pursuit of different prey. Should one have the ill grace to do so, one is expected to pour effusive apologies upon the hapless rodsperson as well as offer some of the better morels as recompense. No need to worry, gentle reader, the offer of an unknown wild mushroom will not appeal to any who would choose to fish when there are Morels Out There.

One must be equally considerate of the illegal Elk Hunter. One is expected to wear much Day-Glo Orange and generate much hue and cry during the Morel Stalk. Nothing is as disconcerting to a poacher as to have to decide between reporting a dead body now, with the accompanying falsehoods, or later—after the smuggled elk has been secured. The morel stalker should not inflict such decisions on others. Many may take Ms. Mushroom to task, but Ms. Mushroom stands fast in her conviction that Noise is Essential in mushroom manners and one's continued survival.

8. One shall not overstate one's good fortune. No matter that one has an entire pick-up load of morels to process for future use. One is only permitted to allude to having found a "few" morels this past week and to state that knowing one's friend might be wanting some, one would like to take this opportunity to share. Not only does this induce in every acquaintance a warm feeling of friendship, but one appears benificent while simultaneously retaining a goodly number of the morels garnered. (One will of course be certain to include at least one or two prime specimens with the less fortunate.)

9. The gentle reader who does not have the good fortune to find as many morels as one would have wished must also behave with grace. One is not permitted to whimper piteously about the time and expense devoted to a vain search nor may any tears be shed when viewing the bounty of the more fortunate. One must maintain a stoic demeanor at all times with one exception: One IS permitted a small moan of awe and a quiet, "I've never even *found* a morel before; yours are so pretty." Sometimes the benificent hunter will share the booty. (It is important that one not allude to the hundred morels one has already secured in one's home refrigerator.)

10. When one returns from a morel stroll, it is considered bad form to tell anyone, even one's nearest and dearest relative, the precise location of one's find (should one prove successful). The precise location of one's find is defined as anywhere within sixty miles of the actual excursion. A simple "Up in the Adirondacks" will do in answer to curious inquiries. Also one never, ever, returns to that spot without first asking permission of the person who introduced one to that spot, nor should one break an unspoken troth by ever asking the host whether one might bring a third party to that location, as this is considered a Breach of Promise. While there may not be mushroom claims registered with the State Land Bank, one must refrain from imposing on one's gracious host. Also, one should know that Mushroom Etiquette encourages Instant Reprisal. If one has broken any of the above rules, one's former host, even though previously one's nearest and dearest companion, may evince only a lingering hint of wistfulness while adjusting the noose over an Oak in the center of the morel patch.

The following recipe is reprinted with permission from *Old-Fashioned Mushroon Recipes* © 1981 by Bear Wallow Books. This makes an exciting first course for dinner or an entire lunch. (See page 109 for ordering information.)

Morel Mousse
(serves 4-6)

1 pound fresh morels
2 T. melted butter
2 T. flour
4 egg yolks, beaten
½ tsp. salt
¼ tsp. paprika
½ cup whipping cream
2 egg whites, beaten stiff but not dry

Chop morels finely. In a medium saucepan melt butter and sprinkle in chopped morels. Sprinkle the flour over them and gently saute the morels (2-4 minutes). Let cool. In a small bowl beat egg yolks with salt and paprika and beat into the sauteed morels. Whip cream until stiff peaks form. Then fold into morel mixture. Next fold in the egg whites. Pour mixture into a buttered 9-inch ring mold and cover with a sheet of waxed paper smeared with butter. Place mold in a pan of hot water. Bake approximately 60 minutes at 325 degrees (preheated). When done, carefully hold mold upside down over serving platter and quickly slide buttered paper from beneath, allowing molded mousse to slide onto platter. Fill the inner ring with your choice of hot buttered vegetables.

Part 3
"We found a few. . ."

Thank you Alice Strand of Pinewood, Minnesota, for this fine morel soup suggestion.

Morel Cheese Soup
(serves 6)

4 cups water
1 tsp. salt
¼ tsp. cumin
1 bay leaf
3-4 medium potatoes, diced
2 stalks celery, chopped
2 large carrots, sliced
1 cup boiling water
3 or more cups dried morels
4 T. butter, divided
1 medium onion, chopped fine
6 T. flour
1½ -2 cups milk or light cream
1 green pepper, chopped
chopped chives or parsley
2 T. nutritional yeast (optional)
2 T. tamari or soy sauce (optional)
salt and pepper to taste
2 cups grated sharp cheddar cheese

Cook potatoes, celery and carrots in 4 cups of water with salt, cumin and bay leaf until barely tender. Place morels in a pan with 1 cup boiling water. Cover, remove from heat and let stand for five or ten minutes, stirring occasionally. Drain and reserve liquid. Chop morels if you like, and saute them with the onion in 2 T. of the butter until onion becomes soft. Add remaining butter to onion and morels. Stir in flour and continue stirring until the flour is lightly toasted. Add enough milk or cream to the morel liquid to make 2½ cups of liquid. Stir liquid into morel mixture with a wire whisk. Continue stirring for a couple minutes, then pour into the pan of vegetables. Add green pepper, chives, yeast, tamari and salt and pepper. Simmer gently for 10 minutes. Remove from heat and stir in cheese. Serve at once or let sit for awhile to increase the morel flavor.

"Those are beauts...I know people who have driven all the way from New York to Michigan for morels and found fewer than that."

This entry from H.M. Marty of Phoenix, Arizona uses morels with a good beer batter.

Fried Morels a la Iowa

1-1/3 cup flour
1 tsp. salt
dash of black pepper
1 T. melted butter
2 eggs, slightly beaten
3/4 cup milk or beer
lots of butter for frying

All the morels you can eat, washed and sliced

Mix together the flour, salt, pepper, melted butter, eggs and milk or beer. Batter should be thick enough to coat the morels nicely. Fry in butter until golden brown. You may keep adding to the batter, depending on how long the morels hold out.

Pleasant Valley (Excerpt)
Louis Bromfield

The American novelist and author Louis Bromfield (1896-1956) was born in Mansfield, Ohio. He served in France during World War I and lived there in the 1920s. In 1933, he purchased a 1,000 acre farm near Mansfield, which he named Malabar. Some of his best known later works, including Pleasant Valley, *are accounts of his farming experiences.*[1]

Like sugar making, the arrival of the morels marks a stage of spring and the hunt for them has long since become a sort of rite among all the country people of the Valley. The morels come not at the turn of the season but in May when the woods and thickets and orchards and pastures are at their most beautiful. There is no special date for their arrival since like the flow of maple sap, it depends upon the season. If you are an old morel hunter you smell the arrival of the fungi in the air. They appear as the last of the Dutchman's-breeches and trillium are fading and the May apples have not yet begun to flower.

I am always astonished at the number of people who are ignorant not only of the delicacy of the morel but even of its existence, although in parts of the East and nothwestern states the morel is fairly abundant. In France where certain of the family grow, their season is an event in the year of the epicure and some eat them twice a day during the week or two they appear in woods and orchards and pastures. For myself I place them at the very top of all delicacies, above *pate de foie gras* and salmon trout and *ecrevisse*, far above the ordinary well-known mushroom whose flavor is strong and coarse by comparison. Although country people continually call them mushrooms, they are not proper mushrooms but belong to another species of fungus and according to the very sketchy three-line account in the Encyclopaedia Britannica they are called *Morchella Esculenta* and belong to the genus *Ascomycete*.

To any but an expert on fungi none of this means very much and I suspect from the immense lack of information on the subject even the experts know little about them. Certainly I have been unable to find any description of the five different varieties or forms which come up each spring at Malabar. Four of the forms bear a resemblance to each other and may be simply variations altering their form and color according to the amount of sun and moisture or the quality of the humus out of which they grow. All of them are gray or yellowish-gray and resemble a cluster of brains or tripe borne upright in the form of a conical cap on a squat hollow stem. One variety, the earliest, is small and firm and rubbery in texture and is found only in our blue-grass pasture where the forest had been cleared away. The next to appear is a yellowish-gray fungus of the same form but more yellow and loose in texture. They seem to flourish in old apple orchards. Latest of all come the yellow and black giants which resemble the others and are found only in the deep woods where the shade is thick and usually in the vicinity of ash trees.

There is a fifth kind which may easily be a totally different species. It grows in deep woods and thickets, a great hollow white stem capped by the prettiest of tiny cones of a rich brown striped with black. These are known locally by the homely and descriptive name of "dog pecker." All this observation is at first hand and scientific as far as it goes, and I have been unable to unearth much more information concerning them. From my observations the "dog peckers" and at least two of the variations exist only on this continent. No one has found any means of growing them artificially and this fact increases not only their value but the excitement of the epicure during the few days when they are available.

The hunt for them during a week or two in May is one of the excitements of the year which engages everyone on the farm from the grandmothers and full-grown men to the smallest boy. There is always an acute rivalry about the finding of the first morel and the boys sneak away from the plow into the woods and my mother goes poking about the old orchard with her stick in search of them days before they are due to appear. Then one day someone announces he has found the first ones and produces three or four in a hat or out of the pocket of a shirt. And the hunt is on!

The peculiar excitement of a morel hunt is not quite like any other excitement I know. Perhaps there is in it something of the beauty of the season itself when the woods and orchards and pastures are moist and damp and dripping and smell not only of wild flowers but of the clean tangy scent of decaying leaves. And there is the bright weather of May when the warm showers fall on you, soaking you through, producing no feeling of discomfort but on the contrary one of great satisfaction as if you yourself somehow drank in the warm shower through your skin and had become a part of the whole rebirth of the world. And the morels are very difficult to see for in the sun and the shadow of the decaying leaves and grass from which they spring, their range of browns and grays serves to hide them as a leopard hidden in the jungle. And each one of them is a beautiful thing in its delicacy and moistness, beautiful to look at and smell and touch. And there is something mysterious about them and the quickness of their sudden appearance. I have returned after a couple of hours to a spot where I have picked every morel to find a whole new crop sprung up. Bob says, half joking, half in earnest, that he believes they spring up the moment your back is turned.

For a few days, while they are in season, everyone at Malabar spends an hour or two a day looking for morels, and for these few days everyone eats morels with steak or broiled or creamed on toast. Sometimes if the season is cool and dry, they are scarce and perhaps only a handful are found during the whole season. In the springs of 1943-1944 which were warm and wet after cold, dry winters, they appeared in abundance over all the country.

Sarah J. Dennett of Iowa City, Iowa suggested the following recipe.

Manistee Morels

3 T. butter
1 onion, diced
½ pound morels, cleaned and sliced
4 T. flour
1/8 tsp. thyme
¼ to ½ cup sour cream

Saute onions in butter. Remove from pan and saute morels in remaining butter. Stir in flour, add onions and thyme. Saute a minute or two together. Add sour cream and heat to a simmer. (it will thicken slightly). Serve on toast or with grilled steak. Manistee morels can also be baked in a cream cheese dough and served as an appetizer.

Pastry

½ pound cream cheese
½ cup butter
1½ cup whole wheat flour

Blend all ingredients and chill for at least half an hour. Roll dough very thin, (1/8"), cut in 3" circles and place a small spoonful of morel filling on each circle. Fold in half and seal the edges with a fork. Bake on a cookie sheet at 450 degrees for about 15 minutes, or until lightly browned.

"No damn way will I ever take anyone to that spot."

Thank you to Geoffrey Larson, of Northfield, Minnesota, for his idea of using leftover cheeses and morels as a late night supper.

Morel Fondue
(serves 4-6)

2 cups morels, chopped
2 T. butter
½ cup colby cheese, shredded
½ cup swiss cheese, shredded
½ tsp. dry mustard
¼ cup sherry

Saute morels in butter until the juice evaporates. Puree morels in a food processor or blender. Pour the puree into a fondue pot and add sherry. Heat mixture until bubbly. Add shredded cheeses and dry mustard to the pot and stir until melted. Serve with lots of cubed French bread.

Lovely Morels in Indiana
Gretchen Leicht Lamberton

For many years, Gretchen Leicht Lamberton's column "The Casual Observer" appeared in the Winona Daily News *and later (simultaneously)* The St. Paul Sunday Pioneer Press. *After her passing in 1965, some of her columns and recipes were collected in* Reflections and Recipes *(Winona, Minnesota: The Leicht Press, 1966). Reprinted with the kind permission of her daughter, Dare L. White.*

PERU, IND.—The main reason I'm down here on Fountain Glen farm right now is because the morel season is in full swing. As many people know, morels are the lovely pale-tan spongelike mushrooms that grow for just two weeks in May. Morels cannot be cultivated or domesticated but apparently grow only in the Middle West and central U.S. and in France, Germany and Belgium. In Europe they are rated as the world's top delicacy, outranking caviar, truffles, trout, etc. During the two-week season in France wild morels from the forests and meadows are rushed to Paris and may be ordered at the two or three greatest restaurants in town— at a price. In Germany, laws had to be passed forbidding the burning over of wooded land for the encouragement of morels.

Morels are one of nature's mysteries. Scientists have never been able to propagate them, and they grow capriciously in old orchards, meadows, sunny clearings or muddy banks—if they feel like it. Sometimes they appear in the same spots year after year, and sometimes they don't. The exactly right time for morels is after the very earliest wild flowers have bloomed—when the hepaticas are just finishing up and the May apples and wild bluebells are starting to bloom. In Indiana this is the first two weeks in May. In Minnesota it seems to be the last two weeks of May.

When I was a small girl I used to pick morels with my grandmother, but for years they have been exceedingly scarce around our Winona area. But this part of Indiana abounds in them, and during these two weeks the entire population goes morel hunting every spare moment. Along country roads cars are lined up with people roaming the nearby pastures and rolling hills with baskets or sacks.

There are several kinds of morels. The earliest are small pale-gray conical sponges about the size of robins' eggs on hollow stems, and they are really difficult to spot as they poke their heads up through dead leaves. Then in a few days the big king morels appear—larger creamy-tan sponges shaped like small Christmas trees with hollow trunks. The rarest are the black king morels, large blackish sponges. All have the same exquisite flavor.

****

The natives call morels "sponge musharoons" and they keep exact count of the number they find and trade information about the numbers—but never the exact location (like trout fishermen). When I got off the train my son's three children greeted me with "Just think, grandma! We found the first morels, 93 of them, in our woods this afternoon and we're going to have them for dinner tonight!" Walking through a pasture that evening, my son found 50 more, so we had 143 morels fried in butter that night.

The next day my daughter-in-law, pre-kindergarten Sara, the two golden retrievers and I walked up into the woods, a 180 acre hill forest of towering virgin timber carpeted with deep moss, ferns, hepaticas, bluebells and other low-growing flowers. Scattered around were patches of taller May apples, blue phlox and a sort of red trillium that I didn't know.

In the sunnier clearings we came upon a few little gray morels poking their heads out of the moss and gray leaves, and it was a thrill rather like finding a lion's paw shell on a deserted southern beach. We found 92 within 15 minutes, then not another one in the next hour or so. Later in the day we found 109 more, and that night we had 201 morels delicately fried in butter. Out of this world!

Hunting morels is a lovely and exciting thing. In my son's woods the ground was ankle-deep in flowers, and sunlight filtered through the giant trees; wood thrushes sang their lovely chiming song, and the air was a tapestry of songs of birds I didn't know.

That day the temperature was in the 80's. But the next day we had tornado winds and chill rain, so did not hunt musharoons. But the following day, last Sunday, I got up early, breakfasted at 5:30 with my son and left with him in his truck on a 34-degree morning. While he fed the steers at the steer barn I climbed the nearby slope and found several of the big tan king morels. Even that early on a Sabbath morning the roads were full of parked cars of musharoon hunters.

After an hour my son drove up the hill to fill the cattle watering tanks in the upper pasture. A cold rain began to fall, and it turned to slushy snow. But we searched the hill and pastures for morels, with fairly good luck, until we were soaked to the skin and thoroughly chilled. A new experience, hunting musharoons in a snowfall. Many demon musharoon hunters stayed out most of the day.

****

It's impossible to describe the flavor of morels. They are exquisite and absolutely unique, that's all, and they should never be cooked in fancy ways but just fired in butter.

When I think back to my childhood and remember the many springtime meals we had consisting of my father's freshly caught brook trout, peeled fresh white asparagus and fried morels I can only marvel at the way we children took these rare delicacies for granted. Since morels are fairly perishable and fragile I shan't try to take any fresh ones home from Indiana. But we are stringing a few and drying them in the sun as the pioneers around here used to do.

Beth Hoven Rotto of Decorah, Iowa suggested the following recipe.

Morel Stroganov
(4 servings)

1 cup dried navy beans
4 cups water
1 cup chopped onion
¼ cup butter
3 cups morels, halved

¼ cup unbleached flour
1/3 cup sherry
1 tsp. salt
2 tsp. dry mustard
2 tsp. worcestershire sauce
¼ tsp. ground nutmeg
1½ cup yogurt (or part sour cream)

Soak navy beans in water until soft. Drain and save the stock.
Saute onion in butter, add morels and cook until soft. Stir in
flour and cook, stirring for 2 minutes to make a roux. Stir in
1-1/4 cup of bean stock, sherry, salt, dry mustard, worcestershire sauce, nutmeg. Cook until thick. (It will be very thick
at this point.) Stir in cooked beans. Remove from heat and add
yogurt or part sour cream. Serve over cooked bulgar wheat or
rice or toast or egg noodles.

"I really like them. . .I could eat them once a day,
every day."

Of Men and Morels
Peter Canby

*This account of the "22nd Annual Mushroom Hunting Champion-
ship" appeared in* Audubon, May 1982. *1981 was the second year
of the "Tony Williams era," which lasted through the 1984 Championship. In 1985, Tony retired from competition. . .at least tem-
porarily. Reprinted with permission from the author.*

The spring of 1981 was a season of great anticipation for mushroom hunters in Boyne City, a small lower-peninsula Michigan
town that for the past twenty-two years has hosted the National
Mushroom Hunting Championships. The 1981 championship was
expected to be a showdown between two local heroes. Dana
Shaler, thirty-two, a tall, bearded millwright and four-time champion, was scheduled to meet, head to head, his arch rival, Stan
Boris, twenty-nine, equally large, a plumber by trade, all-time
record holder, a six-time champion.

Boyne City is the self-proclaimed mushroom capital of the
world, but the contest it sponsors concerns itself only with the
family Morchellaceae, or morel. This should not be surprising.
Morels are the most elusive and prized of the edible fungi. They
are found over much of the country but flourish in few places the
way they do among the rolling hills, hardwood forests, and farms
around Boyne City.

Local wisdom has it that morels are found around stands of
poplar, or at the bases of dying elm trees. They are also said to
grow in apple orchards and in burnt-over forests of all kinds, but
these are the most general of rules and, in Boyne City, there are
many exceptions. It also seems safer to observe that morels are so
unpredictable that no one without local experience can say where
they will grow from year to year. One Michigan mycologist, re-
flecting on the difficulty of definition of morel habits and classification, told me: "At a certain level it is pure opinion.Discussing
morels over a few beers can be as accurate as discussing them when
you're fully sober." Little did I know how apt this observation
would prove when, in early May of last year, I set out to pay visits
to the two champions—Dana Shaler and Stan Boris—to reap the
benefits of their respective insights.

Stan Boris, although a native of Boyne City, lives in the nearby town of Charlevoix. He carries a business card that reads: STAN BORIS. MUSHROOM GUIDE. MUSHROOMS FOR SALE BY THE BUSHEL. Across the top is written, I BUY LIONEL ELECTRIC TOY TRAINS. I telephoned Boris and arranged to meet him late one afternoon in Charlevoix.

Boris lives in a green-and-white trailer set on the edge of the road on top of a long, sloping field overlooking Lake Michigan. I was already at the Boris trailer with his wife, Gerry, and a five-year-old son, John, when Boris got back from work. He came in the door wearing a blue windbreaker with *Plumbers & Pipefitters Local 639* written in big yellow letters across the back. Boris is big, hulking, bushy-haired and generally unshaven—entirely unlike any mushroom hunter I had ever imagined. He said nothing as he entered but glanced briefly at me out of the corner of his eye, like a whale swimming past an underwater camera, peeled off his jacket, took a tall bottle of Coca-Cola out of the refrigerator, pulled on a candy-striped, short-brimmed cloth hat, turned to me, stared ominously, and pronounced in a loud voice, "Well, I'm ready."

Boris drove me to a young poplar-maple-beech forest not far from his house. "The way I generally get mushrooms," he explained as we drove, "is to get my chainsaw running at the edge of the woods. I put it on the ground while it's still running so that the mushrooms think I'm cutting wood. I sneak up, pick off the lead mushroom, then round up the rest." Boris laughed loudly at his own joke.

We got out of the car and Boris led the way into an area of long ridges several hundred feet high which were covered with an open hardwood forest. He picked up a long staff from the forest floor and strode off confidently. He was wearing a faded black-and-white-checked flannel shirt and jeans. The jeans hung below his large belly, low on his hips. The empty Coke bottle was thrust jauntily into his back pocket. "I walk at a steady three miles an hour," Boris told me. "I try to spot the mushrooms twenty or thiry feet out. You lose them close up. If I don't see any, I keep moving until I do. They often grow close together, so when I spot one I stop and examine the surrounding area. The main thing is that if you want to find any you've got to keep moving."

Boris explained that the blacks were out and growing in low points along the ridges, where the forest floor was damp but not swampy and where there was a lot of green. "It's been a dry spring," he observed. "They're growing in the places where the snow last went out." He stopped and pulled up a small lily-like plant that was around in great numbers. He peeled back the lower stem and told me to take a bite. It tasted like raw onion. "That's a wild leek," he told me. Boris sniffed the air skeptically. "See how the air is different around here? You can smell the leeks in the air. If I were a mushroom I'd want to grow here."

Boris soon began to find mushrooms. But, even mindful of his advice, I was having trouble spotting the morels against the forest floor. I couldn't help looking under my feet, and the effort of scrutinizing so many details made me dizzy. After ten or fifteen minutes, I had one morel in my bag—a black, *Morchella angusticeps*— which I had spotted backlit along a ridge above me, glowing in a shaft of late-afternoon sunlight like a jack-o'-lantern. Boris looked at my one mushroom, rattled his several dozen, and asked, "Are you going to pick or just stand around watching?" We were near the top of one of the ridges. Boris leaned down and picked a black morel beside a poplar root about a foot away from my right shoe. He dropped it condescendingly in my bag. "That one would have tripped you if I hadn't gotten it." I looked down and noticed a mushroom behind the spot where Boris was standing. I picked it up and dropped it in his bag. He frowned. "There's two things I want to impress on you," he said. "The first is always to hire a guide—and I'm the only one I know. The second is never, never, never find a mushroom behind your guide."

A few hours later we returned to Stan Boris' trailer with a few hundred morels—mostly blacks— and a few *Verpa bohemica*, which Boris and other Boyne City residents call "caps," because their caps hang away from their stems like half-furled umbrellas. Boris sat me down with his young son John at one end of the kitchen table while he ate his dinner of fried bologna and boiled potatoes at the other. Under his watchful eye John and I were to clean the mushrooms. We carefully separated the *Verpa bohemica*, which Boris' family would eat, from the marketable *Morchella*. Young John asked me if I wanted to hear a new record of his. He ran into the next room and put it on. It was "Whistle While You

Work." We split and washed the mushrooms. Stan's wife, Gerry, sauteed some of the *Morchella* in butter, and I sat and ate a mound of fresh, wild morels while a chorus of Disney woodland creatures whistled cheerfully in the background.

I met Dana Shaler the next day—the evening before the first round of the mushroom contest. Once again I had preceded my guide to the rendezvous, and when Shaler came in, I was sitting at a corner table in Betty's Good Food Restaurant in Boyne Falls eating a piece of homemade lemon-cream pie and eyeing an Amish family at the table nearby. They were as sharply etched and as still as a Vermeer—the father bearded and rigidly immobile, the eyes of the wife and two children darting about nervously. They sat in severe and strained silence. When Shaler joined me I asked about the family. He told me that since the Amish do not drive, these probably had hired a driver to bring them up from Indiana so they could pick mushrooms. "They pick from daylight to dark," Dana told me. He recounted asking a group of them how they'd done. "Not bad," they had told him. "We had five or six bushels at the end of the day."

Dana Shaler is a solid, well-built man with a thick beard and a deep tan. As a millwright, working—when he can get work—at $13.01 an hour, he installs compressors, generators, elevators, and conveyors—"anything that moves," as he puts it. But this work is a recent calling, and precision is the connecting thread in his extensive previous work history: machining, tool and die and masonry. Dana Shaler had won the mushroom-hunting contest three of the last four years. In 1980, the fine-tuned Shaler mushroom machine was thrown off by a last-minute wisdom tooth extraction and he finished seventh. But he expressed the hope that this time he would be able to regain his title by using his superior experience and finesse against his younger competition.

Shaler got a cup of coffee to go, and we set out for some state land up behind Boyne Falls. We drove up old logging roads along meandering stream beds, through brilliant green fields, budding hardwood stands, and past wild cherry trees in full bloom. It is one of Shaler's proud boasts that he can spot morels from a car moving fifteen or twenty miles an hour. "I've got good eyes," he explains modestly. Shaler did himself one better. With the truck going off the deep end," with a cup of coffee sloshing in one hand while the other was steering around enormous mounds and deep ruts in the road, he was still able to spot a group of morels around the base of a stand of dead elms near the roadside. We got out to look. The three he had spotted turned into a dozen, then two or three dozen, until we had found seventy or eighty in all. They were white morels, *Morchella esculenta*, which tend to cluster more than the blacks. Shaler took out his metal lunch pail and filled it two-thirds of the way up. He looked delighted. "Before this I'd have said that two hundred would have won the contest tomorrow. It's been dry and too cold at night, but with the whites out I'd say it might be more like three or four hundred."

I asked Shaler what his strategy for the contest was. "I generally run out a mile or so to get away from people at the starting point. Then I start prospecting. The main thing is to cover enough ground. I pick a lot of them on the run."

I asked him if he ever got lost. "I never have," he said, "but it happens. Last year Ed Crozier came running over a ridge, and just over the other side was a black bear. Ed froze. The bear came toward him. Ed ran. He didn't stop until he was clear to Petoskey. He flagged down a car when he reached a road and the driver made him trade all his mushrooms for a ride back to Boyne City." Shaler paused and then added, "At least that's how Ed tells it."

A spring drive on a muddy Boyne City logging road can yield as many as a dozen pickup trucks an hour, all driven by local people hunting for morels. Fresh morels in northern Michigan bring something like $7 to $9 a pound; dried ones, $50 to $100 a pound. Although this is not money to scoff at in a rural town, the morels are hard to find, and the cash does not begin to pay for the time it takes to hunt and clean the mushrooms.

The champion of the Boyne City contest achieves a certain local prestige, but there are many local mushroom hunters too busy hunting on their own to enter the contest. Under whatever circumstances they are hunted, however, the morels around Boyne City seem to have an almost mystical hold on the local populace. It is possible that this is rooted in the mushroom's biological role, since fungi seem to exercise a fascinating contempt for the diurnal regimens of green plants. This role is to break down organic compounds, thus making them reusable in simpler forms. The late mycologist Louis Krieger argued that without this fungal process the soil would soon be exhausted and "the remains of plants and animals...would, in a short time, clutter the Earth to such an extent that there would be no getting about."

Morels grow in such a variety of conditions, and in such diverse shapes and colors, that what is true for one species of morel in one place may not be true in another. Morels that grow in Boyne City under elms and poplars are found under pines in the Pacific Northwest. Local people know that they are dealing with something elusive, and that—more than money or local fame—enhances their interest in morels. At the mushroom festival there is a souvenier T-shirt that graphically illustrates some of Boyne City's feelings toward the morel. It shows a leprechaun peering out from behind a giant morel, and it bears the caption: "Boyne City, Wild and Free."

The day of the first round of the Boyne City morel championship was overcast and cool. The town's two motels were crowded, and the state parks were full of campers. At 9:45 a.m. all mushroom hunters mustered in the Boyne City High School parking lot, from which they were to proceed, in automobile convoy, through the town and on to secret, undivulged hunting grounds. There were about a hundred cars, most of them with several mushroomers. I parked my car in one of a number of parallel rows and noticed Dana Shaler off to one side chatting confidently with a group of well-wishers. Within a few minutes the row next to mine began to fill up. I watched in my rearview mirror as a huge, ugly, rusted brown Chrysler Newport nosed its way into the space next to mine. There was a loud derisive laugh. I looked up, startled. "Don't get in my way," said Stan Boris. "I'd hate to have to make tracks up your back."

Moments later the Boyne City chief of police leaned on his car at the front of the assemblage, pulled his mike off the dashboard, and informed us of our route. "Do not stop at stop signs or stoplights. You have this right," he squawked. Sirens wailed, and whistles blew. The convoy got under way gradually, formed into a line that must have been a mile long, and proceeded slowly through town. Store windows were painted with giant morels. Grandmoms in rockers waved from porches. Octogenarians with dripping ice cream cones stared in amazement. Kids on Schwinn bikes with baseball bats on their shoulders counted out-of-state license plates.

Ten miles later, the convoy came to a halt in a large field surrounded by wooded hills deep in the Jordan Valley State Forest. The chairman of the mushroom festival announced the rules of the contest. There were ninety minutes in which to pick mushrooms. Anyone returning after the end of the contest would be docked mushrooms. Any contestants who returned to their cars before turning in their mushrooms would be disqualified. Everyone was then issued a numbered shopping bag from which the totals would later be counted.

There was a palpable nervousness in the air. Stan Boris and Dana Shaler were on one side of the crowd, shaking and stretching their limbs like sprinters before a track meet and eyeing each other as if each were afraid the other would get out of his sight and reap some windfall harvest. A shotgun was raised and fired, signaling the start of the contest. For a brief second the action seemed frozen. Stan Boris was suspended in mid-leap, with his numbered bag at his side, like a shopper at a fire sale. Dana Shaler was pointed toward the woods and running, with his chest out, like a Keystone Kop. Then the scene dissolved and the contestants scattered, running at full speed for the hills.

The Boyne City championships are held on two consecutive days. Saturday's round was a preliminary one. On Sunday, winners of several categories were to compete against each other in the mushroom-hunting finals. The Saturday results were satisfyingly close. Dana Shaler had 426 mushrooms; Stan Boris ("It was that last one I decided to leave"), 425. Their nearest rival had 227. That night the town of Boyne City was a social whirl—a Swiss-steak-and-mushroom-gravy dinner at the Order of the Eastern Star, an all-you-can-eat ham dinner at the Vetrans of Foreign Wars, and a Mushroom Hunters' Ball at the New Mogul Inn.

On Sunday the weather was cloudy and raw, and the temperature was in the mid-thirties. A somewhat reduced and subdued parade of finalists from the first round made their way to another

Left to right - Dana Shaler, Stan Boris, and Tony Williams. Boyne City, May 1985.

secret location. This time it proved to be up the Thumb Lake Road behind Boyne Falls—a spot well known, as it turned out, to camping mushroom hunters. Once again it was a hilly region of ravines and ridges covered with beech, maple, poplar and dying elm. Again the mushroom hunters gathered in a small clearing and were issued numbered bags. Again they scattered at a shotgun blast to scour the hillsides and forests, running, bent over with their noses to the ground like bloodhounds on a scent.

But this time, although the mushroom hunters were all there, the mushrooms were not. The champions theorized later that the campers had picked them all, or that the early blacks were almost finished and the cold weather had prevented the whites from coming out in any numbers. In any case the picking was thin, and nobody got much of either kind. Stan Boris, with his flair for the dramatic gesture, came back fifteen minutes early with a disgusted look on his face and a light sack at his side. Dana Shaler came back on time with an even lighter one. An up-and-coming mushroom-hunter, Tony Williams—whom no one seemed to have noticed, and who had won the 1980 contest—weighed in with a comparatively low total of just over 200 mushrooms to take the title.

Williams explained that he had run out at full speed and at only one point had seen Boris or Shaler behind him. He had then run on even farther because, like his older rivals, he had an irrepressible instinct to stay ahead of everyone else. Williams went on to explain that he had learned mushroom hunting from his parents, who had carried him through the woods when he was a baby. He noted also that even though he had won last year's contest, Dana Shaler and Stan Boris hadn't taken him seriously. He was the new kid.

To some, who wanted a resolution of the rivalry between the two champions, the outcome of the 1981 National Mushroom Hunting Championship was unsatisfying. But to most others—especially those who had prior experience with morels—the results merely confirmed the mushroom's already formidable reputation for unpredictability. In Boyne City a bad mushroom year is almost as satisfying as a good one. The important thing, it seems, is the reminder, via the fungi, that nature is complex and that we will never fully understand it. As Gerry Boris observed of the morels, "They're never where you expect them to be, and they're always where you don't expect to find them."

From *Prairie Grass Cooks* recipe book, we selected this recipe using either dried or fresh morels. The combination of morels and Vermouth adds excitement to an otherwise ordinary baked chicken. (See page 110 for ordering information.)

Morel Stuffed Chicken
(serves 4-6)

1 whole fryer, 3-4 pounds
1 pound fresh morels or 1 dozen large dried morels

½ *cup sweet Vermouth*
4 *cloves garlic*
1 *T. minced onion*
2 *T. finely chopped parsley*
4 *T. butter*
1 *cup bread crumbs*
salt and pepper

Reconstitute dry morels in Vermouth. If using fresh morels, soak them in Vermouth for 30 minutes. Dry morels on paper towels and then chop. In the food processor, make a paste of the onion, garlic, parsley and butter. Add morels and bread crumbs and mix. Wash chicken and pat dry. Lightly salt and pepper the cavity of the chicken and stuff with morel mixture. Sew up the opening and bake in a baking dish at 375 degrees for one hour or until leg moves easily from the body. Carve the bird and degrease the juice. Pour juice over carved bird.

From the Harbor View Cafe in Pepin, Wisconsin, owner and chef Paul Hinderlie sent us this recipe for Morels Papalina.

Morels Papalina

Knob of butter
Much garlic, smashed or minced
white Vermouth
1 *cup heavy cream*
pinch of each; white pepper, salt and spice parisienne
morels
pasta
fresh grated nutmeg
fine diced prosciutto
parmesan

Saute garlic in butter. When foam subsides, flame with white Vermouth. Add cream, white pepper, salt and spice. Reduce until thick. Add morels, cook quickly. When done, adjust seasoning. Add prosciutto and serve over pasta. Grate nutmeg over and sprinkle a ring of parmesan around the edge.

Part 4
"Oh. . .oh. . .oh, wow!"

Man finds 20-ounce morel mushroom
Matt Roush

I enjoy Matt Roush's reference to "the sometimes-shadowy world of morel hunting." It's a world of some occasional leg-pulling and, as I consider this article, I'm not just sure to whom the leg belongs. In any event, the photo by Jodee Taylor is bona fide. Reprinted with permission from the June 18, 1985 Traverse City (Michigan) Record-Eagle.

ELK RAPIDS—Robert Morrissey says he has hunted the elusive morel mushroom hundreds of times without luck. But last week he met success—in the form of a 17½ inch tall, 20 ounce giant.

Morrissey found the morel about 10 a.m. June 14 in a bale of hay outside the Morrison Storage Co., four miles north of Acme on U.S. 31, where he works in the shipping and receiving department. "It's the first mushroom I've ever found," the Traverse City man said. "At first I wasn't sure it was a mushroom."

He took it to Tom's Food Market to weigh it, and checked with Guntzviller Taxidermy on how the massive morel might be preserved. He said he heard of a taxidermist in Durand who could freeze-dry it, but said he thought Northwestern Michigan College might be able to do the same thing locally. In the meantime, he said, the specimen is resting its spores in his refrigerator.

Whether or not the morel sets a state record seems as hard to tell as the sometimes-shadowy world of morel hunting itself.

The *Record-Eagle* attempted, through some two dozen phone calls, to determine if the morel is a state record. But neither the state Department of Natural Resources, the state Department of Agriculture, the MSU Cooperative Extension Service, the MSU botany department, the University of Michigan Herbarium nor the Michigan State Library keep records.

Cherry Lake Revisited
Larry Stickney

Larry Stickney is a past President of the Mycological Society of San Francisco and serves as chairman of the North American Mycological Society's Mycogaphy Committee (1985). His article appeared in the MSSF newsletter Mycena News, May 1981; *reprinted with permission.*

August of 1973 campers in Tuolumne Meadows, Yosemite Park saw what looked like a huge fog bank on the western horizon. Another rose at the same time out of the American River canyon, a hundred miles north. Both turned out to be clouds of smoke from huge forest fires. Soon came winter and covered the blackened mountains with snow.

In April of the following year, two adventurous mushroom hunters, Dr. Philip Morgan and Fred Simmons, wandered the Evergreen Road across the Tuolumne River from the burned acreage. What they found astounded them and all those who followed during the next month. Evidence of their discovery first reached the Culinary Group at Stern Grove, when they brought in box load after box load of fresh, clean morels of every size, shape and color. Never had we seen nor eaten so many. Most had never tasted this elegant delicacy; none had ever gorged upon it.

The following weeks were the busiest these morel strewn hillsides had ever seen. The tales sound like the proverbial fish stories one might expect from nearby Cherry Lake. No one who made that long hot drive went home empty-handed. One picked on one's knees and moved only to reach for larger ones or to stretch cramped limbs. The largest single collection, gathered by the Charles Sharp family, amounted to 700 lbs. They brought the largest air-conditioned trailer home they could rent with them—not to sleep in, but to store the hundreds of strawberry boxes of morels under optimum conditions for the journey across the hot San Joaquin Valley. It seemed that all 20,000,000 Californians could not pick all the morels we saw.

There has never been a year like it since, although the second spring yielded good numbers in some spots. By the third year, the best hunting was, and still is, in the Cherry Lake campground where man's disturbing influence still inflicts its damage. For it seems to me that the best moreling is always at 3500-5000 feet on damp ground where yellow pines and cedar trees have recently suffered major or minor root damage.

This recipe is wonderful! Thank you Jim Meads from Glenville, West Virginia.

Morels a l'Escargot

6 large morels
1 clove garlic
½ ounce chopped parsley
½ tsp. Dijon mustard
½ bay leaf, crushed
1/8 tsp. thyme
¼ tsp. ground black pepper
½ ounce lemon juice
¼ tsp. salt
8 ounces butter
¼ cup bread crumbs

Blend together all ingredients except morels and bread crumbs. Cut morels longitudinally into 2 sections and place in an oven-proof dish. Pour mixture over morels and sprinkle with bread crumbs. Broil until butter sizzles. Serve very hot with fresh French bread.

My own book of recipes, *Prairie Grass Cooks*, contains two good recipes using morels. (See page 110 for ordering information.)

Souffle en Roulade with Morel Filling
(serves 6)

12 eggs separated
8 T. butter
8 T. flour
2 cups milk plus 3 T. cream
pinch salt
1 cup grated cheese, either colby or monterey jack
a grating of nutmeg
freezer paper
9½ X 14 jelly roll pan

In a saucepan melt the butter and then slowly add the flour using a whisk to blend. Cook about 2 minutes whisking constantly. Gradually add the milk and cream whisking continuously until sauce thickens. Add the egg yolks and stir for another minute. Add grated cheese and stir over low heat until the cheese has melted. Add nutmeg and taste for salt. Cool mixture. Meanwhile beat the whites until stiff but not dry; they should still have a sheen. Add a small amount of the beaten whites to cool the yolk mixture and lighten the consistency of the sauce, then fold the remaining whites into the yolk mixture. Do this gently but quickly and do not overdo the folding. Prepare the baking pan by cutting a sheet of freezer paper to fit up the edges of the pan with the waxy side up. Pour the souffle mixture onto the paper and bake at 375 degrees for 25 minutes or until lightly golden. Invert the souffle onto buttered foil. Remove the freezer paper and roll up jelly roll style with the foil. At this stage you can let the souffle stand at room temperature for 2 hours or refrigerate overnight. When filling is prepared, unroll souffle, fill it, reroll onto an oven-proof platter and reheat at 350 degrees for 10-15 minutes. The souffle will repuff like magic!

Morel Filling

2 pounds of fresh or 2 dozen large dried morels
1 cup dry white wine
4 cups cream
3 T. butter

If you are using dried morels, reconstitute them by soaking them in the white wine until wine is absorbed. Slice mushrooms lengthwise. Saute in butter in a 2-quart saucepan. Remove mushrooms from pan and add cream. Bring to a boil, then turn heat down so cream is still just boiling but not over the pan. Reduce cream until thick. Add morels and cook together another 5 minutes. Taste for salt. Fill the souffle. Garnish the roll with finely chopped parsley or better yet, chopped basil.

"When they're out, they're out, believe me."

Cleaning Morels
Thomas Dillon Redshaw

This poem celebrates the finding of "a large quantity of morels several years ago." Sadly, not all of them dried successfully. Tom Redshaw teaches English at the College of St. Thomas; "Cleaning Morels" is printed here with his permission.

Crying no farewell, voices fade
down the dry path where dusk springs
first, then creeps up the bank
& streams across the river. Late,
late—the fireflies begin to flash.

Old news of the town clothes
the table & on stigmata of disaster
rest, like aromatic scrolls
from a sandstone cave, morels
dried hollow for a week in the loft.

From black humus understanding
butternut & cherry they plucked
grey morels just where the trail's
most indistinct before the clearing.
Fireflies brighten under the pines.

The serrated knife I begin to ply
has a handle too smoothly green
for any natural thing & a blade
too sharp, like the scalpel
that prunes a tumor, stainless.

Some morels have dried brittle,
black & some leathery, umber under
the blade that lengthwise frees
drugged sawbugs, a panic of ants,
the grey reticule of spider's eggs.

My voices return bearing aurae
of sooty lamplight that blanches
open scrolls to clean gold inside,
yet many wear the hoar of mold
on their skins, so white—too late.

One of three soups we suggest came from Jan Sousa of
Mt. Shasta, California.

Morel Soup
(serves 6)

2 T. butter
1 cup minced leeks (onions if leeks are not available)
1 clove minced garlic
¼ cup minced parsley
minced morels, 1½ cup dried or 2 cups fresh
4 plus cups of water (¼ cup sherry is okay too)
1 potato chopped fine
4 beef bullion cubes
1 bay leaf
salt and pepper

Dried morels should be soaked in 2 cups of warm water until
reconstituted, then save water to use in soup. Saute leeks, garlic,
and chopped morels in butter until soft. Add all ingredients
except potato and cook at a simmer for about 20 minutes. Add
potato and simmer until soup is thickened, about half an hour.
You may like to add other vegetables such as shredded carrots or
celery. Watch your soup to be sure it does not get too thick. If
it does, add more water to suit your taste. Correct seasonings
with salt and pepper.

Monster Morel (Excerpt)
Rodney J. Green

Rod Green is an outdoor writer and an avid morel hunter. This excerpt is from Missouri Conservationist, May 1985, Copyright *1985 by the Conservation Commission of the State of Missouri; reprinted by permission. The photograph, which I like to think of as* The Photograph, *is courtesy of the author.*

A couple of years ago, during the middle of May, I received a telephone call about an unusually large morel found not too far from my home. Driving to the little town of McFall in Gentry County the following morning, I admit I was a bit skeptical. I expected to find a false morel fungus, which looks like a true morel but often grows much larger.

When Ruth Carter opened the refrigerator and produced her plastic-wrapped find, my eyes popped out like a kid's on Christmas morning. There in her hands was an enormous morel—only slightly shrunken and darkened from a night in the cooler. Until that instant, I had thought a morel of eight to ten inches to be a giant.

Like any curious mushroom hunter, I wanted to get the story of how and where the fungus was found. Mrs. Carter, still excited over her find, explained, "Sometime just after noon on Sunday, I opened the door to the crawl space under my house. I keep canna bulbs there, since it doesn't freeze. Just a few feet inside, I caught a glimpse of a strange object. When I saw it, I was startled just for a second, and started to back out. Then I saw it was a mushroom. It astonished me."

I can imagine. I was astonished, too. She had called her son to report the find, but at first she didn't plan to show the morel to anyone. "I just didn't want to brag," she said.

Her son Gary convinced her otherwise and even gave me a call. I would have hated to miss seeing that one. If I ever find one half that size, I will tell everyone, no matter what the circumstances.

Bent in a U-shape from its heavy weight, the morel measured about 22 inches around the outer curve. The fleshy cap, after some dehydration, was nearly nine inches long. A few hours after it was picked, the morel weighed in on the local grocery scales at one pound, 14 ounces.

Much of the rest of the Carter family's Sunday afternoon was spent showing the fungus to local papers and interested outdoors folks. Then in the late afternoon, everybody went mushroom hunting, except Mrs. Carter. "I've found mine already," she said, grinning.

"When I first crept over that fence down there. . .I won't tell you where. . .and saw all those morels, my first thought was, 'This is my last year on earth, and God wants to treat me good.' It was a quarter to ten when I climbed over that fence and started the harvest, and I didn't stand up straight until noon."

Virginia Thornhill of Scottsdale, Arizona sent the following recipe.

Baked Stuffed Morels

3 dozen large morels
2 T. butter
1 T. chopped shallots
salt and freshly ground pepper
1 T. chopped parsley
2 cloves garlic, crushed
½ cup finely chopped cooked ham
3 T. fresh bread crumbs

Clean the morels. Remove stems and halve the caps. Melt the butter in a small pan, add shallots, chopped morel stems and a little salt. Cook until the moisture evaporates. Add a little freshly ground pepper, parsley, garlic, ham and bread crumbs. Correct seasoning with salt. Arrange morel caps in the bottom of a generously buttered baking dish and stuff them with the filling. Bake in a moderate 350 degree oven for 15 to 20 minutes, or until topping is browned.

Another Roadside Attraction (Excerpt)
Tom Robbins

*It would be unfair to attempt a summary of Tom Robbins' wildly
funny first novel here. Obviously any family that hunts morels
with a pet baboon named Mon Cul also operates a unique "roadside attraction." In this exceprt the Zillers introduce the narrator
to morel hunting in Western Washington.*[1]

"The morel is a very wary little mushroom," explained Amanda.
"It hides under fallen leaves as if it were willfully avoiding the
hunter's pluck. Like many of nature's noblest creatures it is a fugi-
tive kind."

The Jeep, piloted by John Paul, was speeding up the river road.
Amanda had executed rough sketches of the morel. She was showing them to Marx Marvelous.

"As you can see, the cap of the morel is shaped rather like a
thimble. A withered thimble. It is pitted, carved with irregular
indentations; honeycombed, as it were. The color of the cap ranges
from tan to creamy brown to a dishwater gray—colors that echo
equally the decaying leaves underfoot and the sodden skies above.
The stem is ivory-white, long and hollow. Frequently, you will
come upon stems alone and you may wonder where the caps have
gone. To the deer, that's where. Morel caps are the deer's spring
tonic. They spurn the stems and leave them standing. We are not
as particular as the deer."

A short distance from the roadside zoo, they had wheeled east-
northeastward off the Freeway and motored for a ways through
fields and pastures of stinging green. Past Burlington, trees grew
more plentiful and there were bright green bogs in which the
skunk cabbage looked like exploding canaries or lemons that had
been hammered into sheaves. After leaving the town of Sedro-
Woolley (site of Northern State Hospital for the Insane), they began to climb, climbing as if the concentrated pressure of those

locked-up crazies was propelling them to loftier altitudes. Higher, higher.

The river was an oxide green and buzzing with silvery silt. If there were fish in it they were well concealed, but occasional steelhead fishermen stood in their flat-bottomed boats, silhouetted in the Skagit mist like mackinawed wraiths. Landward, alders, vine maple and cottonwood thronged down the hillsides to the edge of the road. Where these budding deciduous treelings were mixed with larger, older conifers, there Amanda would point and say, "In April, morels lurked in those groves by the hundreds. The weather is too warm for them now. If we hope to catch morels today, we must go to higher elevations. Even there we won't find many. If we apply ourselves we should get enough for one fine dinner, but this is definitely the last morel hunt of the season."

Marx Marvelous looked over the sketches. He read the morel's botanical name (courtesy of Madame Lincoln Rose Goody): *Morchella esculenta*. He re-examined the drawings. Something dark and ill-defined rustled its arms (or wings or tail) in the hollow behind his heart. He was unconvinced that he wished to dine on these demonic fruits. Morel season could have ended sooner for all he cared. "How can we be sure we aren't picking toadstools?" he asked.

"Specialization is such general tyranny," thought Amanda. "Was it when man initiated the division of labor that he lost contact with the complete reality and began to fragment and go numb? Here we have a scientist, a man who has sacrificed this lifetime to the study of the Earth and its workings, and he does not know that 'toadstool' is just another name for mushroom, edible or toxic. How puny his particular knowledge. Still, I suppose it is necessary. Isn't it?" She thought these thoughts to herself as in her mind's eye she ran naked through the woods, hugging trees.

To Marvelous, she said: "If it is poison you are worried about, you had better stay away from supermarket foods with their preservatives and pesticides."

"Oh, I feel totally at ease in supermarkets," said Marvelous lightly.

You would, though Amanda. Canned peas are not a very potent image. A package of frozen french fries lacks roots that reach into the deep chambers of human consciousness. Ah, but mushrooms! They are standard equipment for sorcerers and poisoners, eh, Marx?

Associated in art, literature and folklore with the wicked and exotic, the mushroom has been used since primitive times to represent death—and death's fair sister, sex. Mushrooms have been called "devil's fruit" and "satan's bread." They do not take to domestication. They lurk in the forest, assume skeleton hues and smell of rot and Pan. Our dear scientist obviously is uncomfortable dabbling in the black arts of yore. She thought these thoughts to herself as in her mind's eye she hugged each further tree trunk, bark and lichen flaking off in green-red scrumbles against her breasts.

To Marx Marvelous she said: "Frankly, there is a poisonous species which is sometimes confused with the morel. It is commonly called the brain mushroom (how Madame Goody refers to it I do not know) and its cap is convoluted like the lobes of the organ for which it is named. That is how one distinguishes it from the morel, in fact. It is folded into many convolutions, rather than depressed as is the morel. If you examine your quarry with this distinction in mind, you cannot possibly make an unpleasant mistake."

"I don't know," said Marvelous, scratching in various places his living statue of natty checks. "Mushrooming sounds to me like a risky proposition."

"A bit like life itself," said Amanda.

****

Although it hasn't rained for two days, the forests are still sopping. The underfooting is spongy, the tree-moss drips and drips. An eerie sunlight filters through the dense tangles of ominously serpentine branches. Shadows are soaked with suggestions of primordial menace and obscure, slinking malignity. White snail shells—some vacant, some stuffed with mucus—are scattered beneath the huckleberry bushes like aquatic curds, and sweating tendrils of ivy choke everything that does not move. In this rank garden of vegetable death, Amanda—more goddess than Hecate herself—rakes the nettles and ferns with her fingers, emitting eeeeeks of minnie mouse surprise whenever she uncovers a treasured fungus. I dread the forest for its universal reminders: it is simultaneously an open womb and an open grave. But Amanda is as at home here as if it were in her own mold that was cast the vast greenfrog jelly of eternity.

Entry—May 10
Notebook of M. Marvelous

****

"Eeeeek!" squealed Amanda, as underneath a great old shaggy-assed cedar she came upon a morel nearly nine inches tall. Earlier, Amanda had told Marx, "The other popular edible mushrooms grow in the autumn. The morel has springtime all to itself." Well, this morel must have had itself one hell of a spring. It was the largest find of the day, the largest of the season. It was a whopper, a prizewinner, a champ, a box-office bonanza, but destined to be dropped right in the basket with the smaller, less glamorous specimens — no star treatment here at Fungus Studios, sorry.

From another part of the woods John Paul materialized, as magicians will, and gave *ex cathedra* sanction to the prize. Even Baby Thor was impressed. He jumped up and down yelling, "Big one! Big one!" Mon Cul caught the fever and slapped his thighs, bowing in the exaggerated manner that he had learned at the Timbuktu Opera. He acted as if the mammoth morel were his own invention, though in truth he had not picked a single mushroom (after all, he was a famous baboon, not some truffle pig). Marx Marvelous had found only about a dozen morels, but with each discovery the thrill increased and he strutted with scientist pride to demonstrate how he had outwitted nature. They were a happy band of food-gatherers, damp and smeared with humus, but happy with the harvest, happy enough to dance, the five of them. And about that time a sudden wild wind gust roared up the Cascade highlands, sounding like a hillbilly hoot, like a Saturday night wahoo; and the shadows grew more tentacular and the sunlight more nocturnal, and the sky thickened like cornstarch and curdled around the tops of the darkening trees. "Let's get home," they hollered, almost in harmony, and singing and chanting four different mushroom hymns in what appeared to be four different tongues (Ziller, as usual, was silent), they Jeeped it on back to the low country, just ahead of the moon.

****

We are driving home by a different route, not following the river back but cutting through the mountains on what is known as the Darrington road. This is logging country, as I ascertain by the bark chips strewn on the highway, by the timber trucks snorting around the twilit curves with one last day's load for the mills. Our own vehicle navigates a curve, and suddenly it is as if we have trespassed into the shattered heart of a no-man's land. Suddenly

there is no more forest. Every hillside, every ridge is bare except
for stumps and slash: a cemetery of forlorn stumps; low-spreading
barricades of rain-rotted, sun-bleached slash. We are in the midst
of an enormous bone yard, a battleground where armies of crea-
tures bigger than dinosaurs might have fought and died. These
murdered hills were for untold centuries green. Deer and bear and
cougar and dozens of smaller animals lived here; eagles nested in
the tops of the firs. Now, they are barren, devastated, splintered,
twisted, silent: not even a magpie sings. They look to be grotesque
Golgothas on which have been crucified a thousand Christs. I am
no lover of the wilderness; the dark, dank woods hold for me a
repertoire of unnamed fears. But if the forest is the product of
satanic forces, then those forces have been surpassed by the grasp-
ings of man. No devil ever dreamed a landscape more terrible than
this.

Entry—May 10

Notebook of M. Marvelous

****

The barbaric spectacle of the logged-off hills stunned them
mute. No one spoke until, stopped at one of Darrington's three
traffic lights, they saw a small crowd of lumberjacks and their
families lined up before a quonset-hut movie theater, waiting for
the show. There were children, some no larger than Thor, licking
eskimo pies; friendly gossip ran along the line from wife to unfas- .
hionable wife; the big men seemed quiet and shy, maybe tired, maybe beaten down by their role in life, their faces already reddened
by the spring sun, their Thom McAn shoes muddy, their jaws shiny
with Aqua Velva—the medicine cabinet stink was detectable as
far as the Jeep.

"They look to be decent folks," observed Marx Marvelous,
"Probably not a guilty conscience among them. Our society *needs*
timber and these loggers are merely doing their jobs. They probably
believe they're performing a patriotic service, and maybe they are.
But I wonder if deep down inside they are completely insensitive
to the brutality of their operation. I wonder if those beautiful
kids will grow up and repeat the slaughter. That is, if there're any
trees left to ravage. I realize, you know, that the logging companies
are replanting. But a tree farm is not a forest. Is it?"

The light went green and the Jeep lunged forward. Amanda
held Baby Thor tightly in one arm while with her free hand she

affectionately fingered morels. Ziller looked over his furred shoulder, first at the logger families in the neoned distance and then at Marx Marvelous. "From little acorns grow the acorn eaters," he said.

****

Morels are ugly in the skillet. The caps look like the scrotums of leprechauns, the stems like the tusks of fetal elephants. Aromatically, the report is more positive. From the pan rises the smell of the whole North Woods stewing in butter. The morels grow friendlier to the nose. But in the mouth, now there is where these dangerous-looking plants really prove themselves. My God, I must confess it: their deliciousness exceeds normal limits of restraint. They taste similar to mealy sweetbreads, to eggplant, to country-style steak, to all three at once. As I munch these delectables, my fearful toadstool prejudices dissolve in a glory of saliva. Perhaps the way to a man's tolerance is through his stomach. Would our relations with China be worse if chow mein were not so popular?

Entry—May 10
Notebook of M. Marvelous

****

While the mushrooms fried and the rice boiled, Amanda prepared a salad, humming while she worked, filling the kitchen with an hallucinatory light, a feminine splendor that jolted Marx Marvelous' imaginative faculties and made him aware of the seraphic appetites in which he professed not to believe. Soon he was on his fifth glass of chablis.

The Zillers, having long ago discovered alcohol to be a most imperfect drug, sipped their wine slowly and repeatedly refused to have their cups refilled. When it became apparent that they would not help him finish the two bottles he had chilled, Marvelous lifted his glass in their direction and asked, "Do you know what Bertrand Russell said about mystics?"

"I do not," said Amanda, ripping the lettuce as gently as if she feared it might cry "ouch." John Paul continued to let jungle murmurings escape his flute.

"Russell said that there is no difference between those men who eat too little and see Heaven and those who drink too much and see snakes." Marvelous leered sardonically into his wine.

"The difference," said Amanda serenely, "is that one of them sees Heaven and the other sees snakes."

94

*In every co-edited book, there will probably be at least one
difference of opinion; we saved ours for last. I think that everyone
should have a "morel sundae" at least once in their lifetime,
while Anne is not so sure. The recipe is from the Phillips Mill
Restaurant near Charlevoix, Michigan; it was sent to us by Jim
Silbar, Editor of the* Charlevoix County Press *in Boyne City.
(I believe that "Vernor's Flavored" ice cream is a Michigan spe-
cialty.) PL*

Phillips Mill Marvelous Morel Sundae
(serves 4)

*3 T. butter
1 cup morels (finely chopped)
1 T. honey
¼ cup pecans (chopped)
½ cup butter
1 cup brown sugar
juice from ¼ lemon
¼ cup Frangelico liqueur
Vernors Flavored ice cream*

Saute the morels in 3 T. of butter. Mix in the honey and pecans.
Stir together ½ cup melted butter, brown sugar, lemon juice,
and Frangelico. Add this to the pecan and morel mixture. Serve
warm over Vernors Flavored ice cream.
This topping is also good on almost any ice cream, cheesecake,
cakes and lots of other desserts, including fresh fruit.

**"I had been hunting mushrooms when I came upon the
body, which was face down." (He added that this was the
second time he had found a body while mushroom hunting.)**

95

Part 5
"Holsome Mushromes that may be eaten."

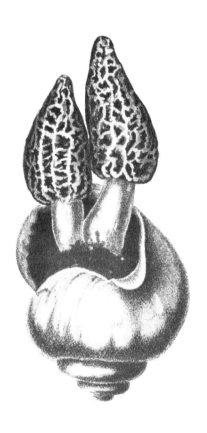

Rariorum plantorum historia   1601   (Excerpt)
Clusius

*Charles de l'Escluse (1526-1609) was known to botanists by the
Latinized named of Clusius. Trained as a lawyer, he became inter-
ested in botany in 1551 and subsequently traveled throughout
Europe. In 1593 he was appointed to the chair of botany at the
University of Leiden, a position he held until his death. I am in-
debted to Jackson Bryce of the Department of Classical Languages,
Carleton College, for his translation from the Latin. The repro-
duction is from the Library of the New York Botanical Garden,
Bronx, New York.*

When I was living in Vienna, Austria, I used to observe many
and various types of mushrooms on my trips into Austria and
Hungary, among which I have no doubt but that the greater part
grow not only in that vicinity, but also in other places; but because it was there that I was able to observe them with especial
care (constantly going forth to meadows, stands of timber, groves
and mountainous and open places, in the company of those who
knew how to discern the harmful and the deadly ones from the
edible), I thought that if I should put together a brief account of
them, I would be undertaking a project not without its usefulness.

I have decided that my work ought to be divided into two
major chapters, so that in the first I may treat of those mushrooms
which are accounted edible and not harmful in the least—although
(as Pliny says) what pleasure is so great as that of possibly dangerous food? In the second chapter, then, I will go through those which
it is not customary to eat, for these are dangerous, even fatal.

CHAPTER ONE: EDIBLE MUSHROOMS

Of the edible mushrooms which I have set out to describe in this
first chapter, there are various genera, and at the same time there
are also diverse specimens of each genus. Now I have thought it
best to offer my account of the individual genera in the order of
the time of year when they appear; and thereafter each genus will
be divided into its species (if it has any).

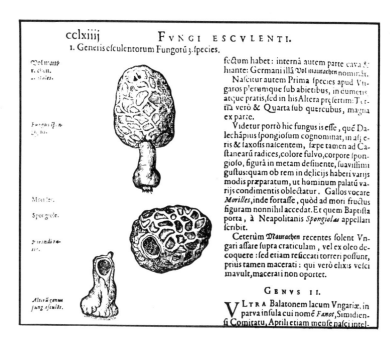

1. Generis esculentorum Fungorū 3. species.

Morchae r. oder ... itales.

Fungus ĩ. ... ...

Morilet.

Sporgele.

Pirandira-...

Alterū genus fungi esculēt.

fectum habet: internà autem parte cava & hiante: Germani illā Vol maurachen nominat.

Nascitur autem Prima species apud Vngaros plerumque sub abietibus, in eumetis atque pratis, sed in his Altera prefertim: Tertiā verò & Quarta sub quercubus, magna ex parte.

Videtur porrò hic fungus is esse, quē Dalechāpius spongiosum cognominat, in alij eris & saxosis nascentem, sæpe tamen ad Castanearū radices, colore fulvo, corpore spongioso, figurā in metam desinente, suavissimi gustus: quam ob rem in delicijs haberi varijs modis præparatum, ut hominum palatū varijs condimentis oblectatur. Gallos vocare *Morilles,* inde fortasse, quòd ad mori fructus figuram nonnihil accedat. Et quem Baptista porta, à Neapolitanis *Spongiolas* appellari scribit.

Ceterùm Maurachen recentes solent Vngari assare supra craticulam, vel ex oleo decoquere: sed etiam resiccati torreri possunt, priùs tamen macerati: qui verò elixis velci mavult, macerati non oportet.

GENVS II.

VLTRA Balatonem lacum Vngariæ, in parva insula cui nomē *Fanot,* Simidiensi Comitatu, Aprili etiam mense nasci intel-

First Genus (Morels)

In April there appears that genus which among the Hungarians and also in Germany is so great a delicacy that they hang them from a nail, strung on a string and arranged in garlands, and thus keep them so as to be able to eat them even in the middle of winter. They are called *szemerchyek* by the Hungarians, *Maurachen* (morels) by the Germans. Four species of this genus are observed, differing among themselves in color and size.

Now the first species rarely exceeds the end joint of the thumb in magnitude, being quite wrinkled, and as it were like a honeycomb, with a membranous outer skin divided into tiny sections. It is of an off-white color as if discolored with soot. Its wrinkles are especially cracked and prominent, and the base it rests on is hollow, as is indeed the entire body of the mushroom.

The second species, not much surpassing the first in size, is a little bit more pinched, and wrinkled like a pear baked in the oven; or one could say that it is the very impersonation of a tuber or root of birthwort, pinched with age and showing many wrinkles. It is of a ruddy, tawny color, wherefore the Germans name it *braune Maurache* (brown morel).

The third, not unlike the first in shape, but twice as big, is most often spherical, except for the base by which it is supported; at the same time, moreover, it grows to a length of three inches, and an equal or greater thickness. It is of the same color as the first species, no less wrinkled than it, and as it were divided into little cavities and hollow on the inside. By the Germans it is called *volle Maurache* (full morel).

The shape of the fourth species, when it has just appeared, somewhat approaches the third, which is spherical, but its wrinkles are more crowded and compressed, as in the second; whereas the color is more whitish and the foot longer. But when it is a little more mature, it grows more elongated just like a cone, or a pointed cap or one of those tallish German alpine hats (but lacking the brim). Its use among the Germans is restricted to winter. It is wrinkled on the outside, and divided into tiny sections, having a somewhat faded color as if discolored with some sort of soot; and on the inside it is hollow and cavernous. The Germans call it *Stock Maurache* (stick morel).

Now the first species grows in Hungary especially under fir trees, in thickets, and in meadows. The second species grows especially in meadows; the third and fourth in great part under oaks.

It seems, further, that this mushroom is that which Dalechapius calls "a spongy mushroom, growing in wild and rocky places, but often by the roots of chestnut trees, tawny in color, with a sponge-like body, its shape ending in a cone, of the most delicious taste; wherefore it is considered a delicacy, prepared in various ways in order to delight men's palates with a variety of seasonings. The French call them *morilles*, perhaps from the fact that they somewhat approach the shape of the fruit of the mulberry" (*mure*). And Baptistaporta writes that they are called *spongiole* (sponges) by the Neapolitans.

Now the Hungarians are accustomed to roast fresh morels on a grill, or to cook them in oil; but they can also be dried, and then roasted after they are first soaked. But those who prefer to eat them boiled need not soak them again first.

Theatrum Botanicum 1640 (Excerpt)
John Parkinson

The Theater of Plantes, *to use its English name, was "Composed by John Parkinson, Apothecarye of London, and the King's Herbarist." This "herbal" contained 1,755 folio pages, over 2,700 woodcuts, and descriptions of more than 3,800 plants. (It is interesting to note that the author also accepted the existence of the unicorn.)*

CHAP. LXIII

Fungiesculenti. Holsome Mushromes that may be eaten.

. . .But I know *Clusius* saith the *Hungarians, Germanes,* and others, doe most esteeme of those that grow in the woods. . .the ordering and dressing them to be eaten is diversly. . .(or) boyle them in milke or creame, or fat broth, others again slice them and strow fine flower on them, and then fry them with butter, suet, or oyle, and so eate them: *Clusius* saith they use in *Germany* to hang them in strings and keepe them dry, others salt them and so keepe them untill winter, (for the best grow up and are gathered in the spring, and not in the Summer or Autumne, yet it is observed that they grow most in a rainy season, and often after thunder) and then dresse and eate them.

1. Some of this kinde grow bigger than others, and some more topped or spiring, and some are parted as it were all over into sundry divisions, making it seeme like unto an hony combe, and therefore are called *Favaginosi,* but are not dangerous as *Gerard* saith, for *Clusius* putteth it as one of his principall or first kindes of edible Mushromes and saith it seemeth to be that which *Dalechampius* called *Spongiosus,* and the *Italians spongiola,* and the *French Morilles,* because the head doth well resemble a Mulberry, and *Camerarius* saith are called *Morchell* by the *Germanes,* who be much delighted with them.

111. Genus esculentorum Fungorum.

Pl. XLVI.

1. 2. **Morchella Esculenta.** (PERS.) Morille comestible.- Spitzmorchel.
3. 5. **Morchella Viridis.** (LEUB) Morille verte.- Grüne Morchel.
(COMESTIBLE. - ESSBAR.)

English Fungi (Vol. II) 1799 (Excerpt)
James Sowerby, F.L.S.

James Sowerby (1757-1822) was an artist and naturalist best known for his English Botany; or Coloured Figures of British Plants... *(1790-1814). In a move toward its present scientific classification, Sowerby suggests here that morels are more akin to false morels* (Helvella) *than to stinkhorns* (Phallus). *Just over 100 years later, Emile Boudier will identify 23 species of genus* Morchella *in his monumental* Icones Mycologicae *(1905-10).*

HELVELLA ESCULENTA.

PHALLUS ESCULENTUS.

This varies a little in shape and colour. Mr. Jacob Rayer found some buff-coloured specimens on a bank in Kent. I have gathered plenty of the blackish kind at Newington, Surrey, on an old garden ground among sugar-bakers rubbish.

This species surely belongs much more properly to the genus of *Helvella* than to that of *Phallus*, especially if we consider its texture, duration, or qualities. It is well known by the name of Morel, and much esteemed as an ingredient in sauces and soups, for which purpose it may be preserved dried for many months or even years. The people employed in gathering Morels in Germany, having observed that they grew most plentifully where wood had been burned, proceeded to promote their propagation by setting fire to the woods, till it was found necessary to forbid that practice by law.

"Everything I've learned in forty years of hunting morels has been disproven."

Journal Entry   1806
Capt. Meriwether Lewis

The Lewis and Clark expedition left Fort Clatsop, Oregon March 22, 1806 on their return journey. Their first attempt to cross the Bitterroot Mountains over the Lolo Pass was thwarted by deep snow. On June 19th, the party was camped somewhere in the foothills to the east of the present town of Weippe, Idaho.

JUNE 19-*Thursday*. The hunters renewed the chase at a very early hour, but they brought only a single fish at noon. The fishermen were more unsuccessful, for they caught no fish, and broke their two Indian gigs. We, however, mended them with a sharp piece of iron, and towards evening they took a single fish, but instead of finding it the salmon of this spring's arrival, which would of course have been fine, it proved to be a salmon-trout of the red kind, which remain all winter in the upper parts of the rivers and creeks, and are generally poor at this season. In the afternoon, the two men who were left behind, in search of horses, returned without being able to find them, and the two other hunters arrived from Hungry creek with a couple of deer. Several large morels were brought in to-day, and eaten, as we were now obliged to use them without salt, pepper or grease, and seemed a very tasteless insipid food. Our stock of salt is now wholly exhausted, except two quarts, which we left on the mountain. The mosquitoes have become very troublesome since we arrived here, particularly in the evening.

Cl... ... .l..o..um Fungorum.

"I've been picking since I was an infant. . .my mom used to take me out in the woods on her back. My family has been in these parts since the logging days a hundred years ago. They've been morel hunters all along, I guess."

British Edible Fungi   1891   (Excerpt)
M.C. Cooke, M.A., LL.D., A.L.S.

After eating morels for the first time, a friend remarked, "You know, I have the terrible feeling I've walked through the woods kicking those things." Some impulses apparently never change, as evidenced in this account from an early English field guide. Reprinted with permission from Routledge & Kegan Paul, London. Note: A "half quartern loaf" would weigh about two pounds.

There are two other, much larger, but we fear much rarer species, which deserve a place in this enumeration. The one species is the great morel *(Morchella gigas)* which has often a stem six inches long and two or three inches thick. The cap is rather conical, free at the edge, and half-way up, two or three inches high and broad. It resembles a gigantic form of the last species, but differs from it not only in size, but also in the scaly stem. It has only been found a few times in this country.

The other, and last, species is Smith's morel *(Morchella Smithiana)* which was at first mistaken for the giant morel or the thick-stemmed morel, and so called when figured in the *Journal of Botany*. The cap is subglobose, tawny, and with deep large pits, the base continuous with the stem. It reaches to a foot in height and seven inches in diameter, with a robust stem. Several instances are known of its occurrence in this country and a single specimen is quite sufficient for a substantial meal. It is remarkable how very persistently a certain class of people, presumably with toes more active than their brains, make war upon unknown fungi, kicking them in pieces, without thought or reason, whenever met with. On one occasion the remains of a splendid specimen of this morel, the size of a half quartern loaf, were found kicked about by some boys, and brought to us for identification. It was a lamentable wreck, but when carefully washed made an excellent meal.

Morels Xeroradiographed   1985
Stanley W. Siegler, M.D.

Dr. Stanley Siegler of Toms River, N.J. is a radiologist by profession and a mycologist by avocation. He uses x-rays generated at a voltage low enough so that shadows are cast of soft tissues which would otherwise be transparent. "It occurred to me that soft tissue 'photography' of mushrooms might be interesting," he says, "since the densities of mushrooms are similar to those of human tissue." In comparing this unique image with that of Clusius' engraver, one might note (to paraphrase Gertrude Stein), "A morel is a morel is a morel."

"I once picked eleven bushels. . .my father told me which ones to pick. You have to look on hills facing south. In Illinois, there were more woods then. All our neighbors ate mushrooms."

"Morel" Etymologized   1986
Peter Leach

It has been my experience that many people are unable to either identify a morel or define the word, referring to *Morchella esculenta*. Many morel hunters, myself included, probably cannot identify the other morel, or black nightshade (genus *Solanum*). With this bit of confusion for openers, it is not surprising that tracing the origin of the word morel gets a bit murky, particularly when you also consider that in French the mushroom is *morille* and the nightshade is *morelle*.

Let me drop mulberries and nightshades from the discussion at this point, noting only that they both appear to be rooted in the Latin *Maur* - Moor, which often connotes darkness (the Italian *morello* means blackish). Most dictionaries show morel being derived from the French *morille*, which is from Old High German (pre-1100 A.D.) *morhila*, from *morh(a)* (or *moraha)*-carrot, plus the diminutive -*ila*.[1] "Little carrot" would not seem to be a bad description of a morel!

---

[1] In discussing the Clusius translation with Jackson Bryce, he suggested that it was unlikely that a French word would be derived from Old High German. His *American Heritage Dictionary* indicates that *morille* is from Old French, from the Vulgar Latin *mauricula*, which might translate as "little dark brown (object)." The final word on this subject may have to await *Malfred Ferndock's Complete History of the Morel* !

107

The foreign words for morel, as listed by Clusius in 1601, are remarkably similar to current usage. The French *morille* remains the same and *Spongiolas* of the "Neapolitanis" has become *spugnolo*. The Hungarian *Szemerchyek* seems related to the Czech *smrz* and Polish *smardz*. Only the German *Maurachen* differs markedly from the contemporary *morchel (Maurachen* is possibly a variation of *moraha)*. John Parkinson, writing in English in 1640, mentions the German *Morchell*, but does not use the word "morel." A century and a half later, James Sowerby writes (1799), "It is well known by the name of Morel. . ."

As I indicated in the Preface, stumbling into the history of morels has been an unexpected pleasure. My only regret is that time did not permit me to explore passing references to morels in colonial America, China (the "Sheep's-stomach mushroom"), Mexico (a source of *morillas deshidratadas*-dried morels), or among American Indians. Whether *you* call them sponges, honey combs, merkles, rooms, or roons, I hope this book will add to your enjoyment of the wonderful morel.

111. Genus esculentorum Fungorum.

Appendix

In the course of editing this book, we found one bit of information here, another item there, and someone else who knew about something. . .if only we could reach them. Here are the results; whether you're a morel hunter, a cook, or just mildly curious, we hope you'll find something of interest.

Cookbooks

There is an almost infinite number of mushroom recipes and the number of mushroom cookbooks is not far behind. This is *not* a complete list by any means, but these seem a little more morel-related than others. We have included a recipe from each; also each of the books is available by mail.

A Judge Judges Mushrooms by Judge Samuel R. Rosen.
A delightful book, covering a variety of mushrooms, with a unique chapter on "The Legal Aspects of Mushrooms."
19 recipes, 96 pages, $7.95 postpaid.

> Highlander Press
> 2454 West 38th Street
> Chicago, IL 60632

Old-Fashioned Mushroom Recipes Bear Wallow Books.
Lots of recipes, ranging from Mushroom Onion Bread to Curried Mushroom Croquettes. . .there are 13 other titles in their Old-Fashioned Recipe Book Collection.
57 recipes, 32 pages, $2.75 postpaid.

> Bear Wallow Books, Publishers, Inc.
> P.O. Box 579
> Nashville, IN 47448

ROON (A Tribute to Morel Mushrooms)
Chelgren-Petermeier-Ratzloff.
The color photographs alone are worth the price of admission. . . they make you want to get into the woods NOW!
12 recipes, 68 pages, $9.50 plus $1.50 postage.

> Cabin Publishing
> P.O. Box 73
> Long Lake, MN 55356

Wild Mushroom Recipes by Carole Eberly.
A wide variety of recipes from the heart of morel country. The Eberlys publish 11 other titles, including cookbooks and Michigan lore. 47 recipes, 64 pages, $1.75 plus $1.00 postage.

> eberly press
> 430 N. Harrison
> E. Lansing, MI 48823

Prairie Grass Cooks by Anne Mikkelsen.
Someone once said to me that functional pottery "doesn't have to be unique. . .it just has to be good." Somehow, this sums up Anne's approach to cooking. . .simple, but very good. If you like the recipes in this book and her approach to cooking, you'll enjoy Anne's own book of general recipes. PL
66 recipes, 62 pages, $6.50 plus 50¢ postage.

> Anne Mikkelsen
> Route 4, Box 212
> Northfield, MN 55057

NOTE: When ordering books, be sure to include state sales tax, if required.

Festivals and Contests

A number of communities sponsor annual "morel festivals." As you might imagine, there are contests, demonstrations, civic celebrations, and. . .MORELS! For further information, write to the following:

> "National Mushroom Hunting Championship"
> Chamber of Commerce
> 28 S. Lake St.
> Boyne City, MI 49712

> "Lewiston Morel Mushroom Festival"
> Chamber of Commerce
> P.O. Box 656
> Lewiston, MI 49756

> "Morel Mushroom Festival"
> Chamber of Commerce
> P.O. Box 127
> Muscoda, WI 53573

The Peoples State Bank of Chandlerville (Illinois) may be the only bank in the country with a cluster of three morels on their letterhead. Their annual "largest morel" contest is based on weight and you must present your entry at the bank for weighing; three cash prizes.

Peoples State Bank of Chandlerville
P.O. Box C
Chandlerville, IL 62627

Malfred Ferndock sponsors an annual "largest morel" contest which is based on height. The entry must be photographed next to a standard 12 oz. beverage can (which is 4 13/16" high); three cash prizes. Contest information upon request; for Malfred's current catalog of unique "morelabilia" send $1.00 (refundable with purchase).

Malfred Ferndock
Box 86
Dennison, MN 55018

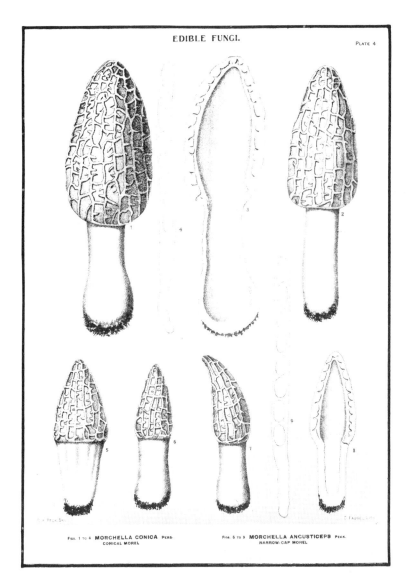

Figs. 1 to 4 **MORCHELLA CONICA** Pers.
CONICAL MOREL

Figs. 5 to 9 **MORCHELLA ANGUSTICEPS** Peck.
NARROW-CAP MOREL

Mycology

When it comes to edible wild mushrooms, morels are merely the tip of the iceberg. (Many morel hunters, being more than a little biased, would point out that the "tip" is also the "top.") Nevertheless, whether your interest lies solely in morels or in the vast world of mycology, you will find much that is of interest from the following sources.

N.A.M.A. is the national organization for mycologists; its membership ranges from professionals to those who like to "hunt mushrooms." (There are about 60 state and local mycological groups; N.A.M.A. can direct you to one in your area.) For membership information:

> The North American Mycological Association
> 4245 Redinger Road
> Portsmouth, OH 45662

Mushroom, The Journal of Wild Mushrooming is a quarterly publication devoted to...wild mushrooming. The Spring issue features morels and subscriptions are $12 a year.

> *Mushroom*
> 861 Harold Street
> Moscow, ID 83843

It would be impossible to begin to list the mushroom field guides which are available. There is, however, a "guide to field guides": *Harper's Mushroom Reference Guide & Check List* "a tabular, alpabetized guide to 1765 species of North American Fungi keyed to 13 leading identification guides."
170 pages, $12.95 plus $1.50 postage.

> Herbert H. Harper
> 8975 North Shore Trail
> Forest Lake, MN 55025

Les Morilles by Emile Jacquetant is simply the most complete, the most beautiful book available on the subject of morels. The text is French, but anyone can enjoy the dozens of color photographs and drawings. It is available from Lubrecht & Cramer, the best single source for mycological books, from field guides to rare scholarly works.

> Lubrecht & Cramer Ltd.
> R.D. 1, Box 244
> Forestburgh, NY 12777

(All of the information above was correct as of March 1986.)

About the Editors

Anne Mikkelsen began cooking seriously after taking classes from Verna Meyer, Minnesota's authority for many years on wine and food. She has had the opportunity to continuously test new ideas and recipes in the restaurant and catering business and on her enthusiastic and encouraging family. Anne received two certificates from classes attended at the Wine Country Cooking School in Napa Valley, California. She has spent invaluable time with Simone Beck in Provence, in the South of France, where not only is technique important, but also attitude.

A professional potter since 1961, Peter Leach produces stoneware for the kitchen and table. He began his career as a morel hunter while growing up in Southern Wisconsin. Regarding this book he says, "Malf still had bits of morel in his beard, from the accident, when he came over and asked if I could help him out. I'm afraid the book may lack some of the humor he would have brought to it, but I've tried. . ."

Acknowledgements

This book was printed by Pauline Redmond and Jack Miller at the Anvil Press in Millville, Minnesota. Divider page drawings (Parts 1-4) by Dorothy Beebee of Forestville, California. Anne Mikkelsen's photo courtesy of the *Northfield News*. Cover photo by Curt Anderson on location at Al's Breakfast Shop in Dinkytown, USA.

MALFRED FERNDOCK'S MOREL COOKBOOK

Please send _____ cookbooks at $8.50   _____
Postage and handling - One book at $1.50   _____
    (Two or more to same address at $2.50)
Minnesota - add 6% sales tax   _____
                          Total enclosed $ _____

Send to:

Name_____

Address_____

City, State, Zip_____

Gift Card: To:_____ From:_____

Mail order to: Malfred Ferndock
                   Box 86, Dennison, MN 55018

- -

MALFRED FERNDOCK'S MOREL COOKBOOK

Please send _____ cookbooks at $8.50   _____
Postage and handling - One book at $1.50   _____
    (Two or more to same address at $2.50)
Minnesota - add 6% sales tax   _____
                          Total enclosed $ _____

Send to:

Name_____

Address_____

City, State, Zip_____

Gift Card: To:_____ From:_____

Mail order to: Malfred Ferndock
                   Box 86, Dennison, MN 55018